For
My
Father's
Daughters

By Deborah Babers

For My Father's Daughters
By Deborah Babers

ISBN 978-1-4303-1994-8

Cover Design by C.Hughes Advertising Agency
Cover Illustration Copyright by pascalepics. Image
From BigStockPhoto.com

All scriptures are quoted from King James Version
or New International Version.

Dedication:

Dedicated to my loving and patient husband, Charles. Your encouragement and loving support have helped to make this possible; and written for my children, Leketia, Samantha, Malcolm & Kaia. I love you all so much.

Acknowledgements:

First and foremost I give glory and honor to my Lord and Savior, Jesus Christ. Without His mercy and grace, I would not be here today. It is through His strength that all things are possible.

I praise and thank God that I have been planted in a church with such a wonderful Pastor. Dr. Mikel Brown, you have indeed been such a wonderful spiritual mentor and teacher. You lovingly bring the timely word, rightly divided, which has been so instrumental in helping me to know God and His purpose for me.

There have been so many other people that have touched my life in order to make this book possible, that I could not thank them all. Thank you, Elder M.E. Campbell, for being the consummate example of a virtuous and loving woman of God. Special thanks to Elder S. W. Whittle: MOG, your edification, patience, and love have been invaluable and intrinsic to my personal and spiritual growth.

And acknowledgement to Jannie Holguin, who, despite her busy schedule, did me the great favor of completing the arduous proof-reading of the original manuscript. God bless you.

Preface

Child sexual abuse is one of the world's more secret crimes. It is an ugly occurrence that most people would rather sweep under the carpet or pretend doesn't happen. It would be nearly impossible to get an accurate count of the number of people who have been sexually victimized, as most people don't report the abuse. The reasons why people don't report are countless: shame, threats, stigma, and social rejection are just some of them.

Because of these, and many other reasons, most of these victims suffer in silence. It may have been years or even decades since the abuse occurred; yet they are still suffering from isolation, pain, and loneliness. They are often functionally depressed, and walk around with the façade that everything is fine. They often feel that they are alone, and that no one around them could ever understand how they feel. Yet their numbers are countless.

The only true way to reduce the number of victims and relieve the pain of those already victimized is to shed some light on the situation. It is never easy for the victims of sexual abuse to speak out about what happened to them. Their hope has often been crushed, and they feel that it is their lot in life. It is because I was a victim, and have since recovered, that I am motivated to write this book. I know that this is a controversial subject that some might find objectionable. This is why, unless it is necessary to demonstrate the mindset I had, the majority of facts have been withheld. It is not my intention to sensationalize my experiences, but to demonstrate the seemingly insurmountable shame and guilt which were the effects of my own abuse.

It is my fervent prayer that you, as the reader, will see that you are not alone. Sexual abuse effects permeate every aspect of a life by way of one's self-esteem. How you see yourself has a direct correlation to the way you treat yourself and the way you allow others to treat you. I pray that you will come to the realization, through Christ, that the abuse was not your fault. Most importantly, I need you to know that what happened to you does not have to define the rest of your life. I am here to tell you that God wants better for you. It is time to break the silence. It is time to make a change. "I can do all things through Christ which strengtheneth me." Philippians 4:13 (KJV)

Table Of Contents

Chapter One

The Seeds Of Destruction.

"Do not be deceived, God cannot be mocked. A man reaps what he sows. The one who sows to please his sinful nature, from that nature will reap destruction; the one who sows to please the Spirit, from the Spirit will reap eternal life. Let us not become weary in doing good, for at the proper time we will reap a harvest if we do not give up." Galatians 6:7-9 (NIV)

The very first realization I had that anything was wrong was at about the age of eight. It was a warm day in late spring. Being eight years old, I was allowed to wander about the neighborhood relatively unchecked. We lived in a small, quiet town. Nothing ever happened. There was very little traffic on our street, and so we had a sense of security there. Our only guideline as children was that we had to be within earshot. Every once in a while we would be allowed to wander farther, but usually only as a group. On that particular day, I had asked for permission to go down a side street (outside of earshot) to visit with an acquaintance. I enjoyed a leisurely stroll down the tree-lined street.

1

The trees towered far above me, their new leaves brightened by the sunlight filtering through them. Recent rains caused a damp fragrance to rise up from the bed of the forestation. Some time later, my friend and I were sitting in front of her house talking, enjoying the warmth of the sunny spring day. My younger brother came gleefully riding up on his bike. The look he had on his face always meant trouble. He took great joy in telling me that I was in trouble. I had to go home right away. Immediately, a sense of dread filled me.

As I made my way towards the house, I could no longer focus on the brilliant sunlight that filtered through the green tops of the trees that lined the street. The usually short walk seemed to become exceptionally long. I felt my legs take on a rubbery, weighted feel. As I reached the bottom of the hill upon which our house stood, I took a deep breath in and forced myself to climb the hill toward the back of the house.

The house we lived in was a split-level home. It was originally built for a wealthy family, and must have been impressive in its day. The house had to have had at least eight bedrooms. It had a large porch on the front that extended the length of the house. A smaller porch lined only part of the back of the house. The dwelling had long since been split to create two separate apartments. Even so, the apartments were quite sizeable. Our family lived on the lower level. There was an expanse of yard on both sides of the house where we often played kickball or softball. There was a huge barn behind the house. It had been remodeled and was occupied by the landlord and his family.

As I reached the rear porch, I had to force my legs and feet to navigate the steps up to the back door of the house. How I hated being in this position. I felt the dread drop to the pit of my stomach as I reached the back door. There was justification for such dread. My father had always been a very strict disciplinarian. Severe infractions of his rules meant severe punishment.

I stood on the back porch. The kitchen windows were open, as were most of the windows in the house. The curtains danced in the breeze running through the house. I opened the door as quietly as I could, slipping in almost silently. From the kitchen entry I could see that, although dusk has approached during my walk home, the lights in the house had not yet been turned on. The house was completely quiet, except for the sound of the television and an occasional cough coming from my father. I could see him, settled back in his recliner, cigarette smoke swirling about over his head.

I remember him most clearly with his posterior parked in that recliner, beer in one hand, smoldering cigarette in the other. In the evenings, he rarely left it, except for a few trips to the restroom. He was a man of massive, imposing stature. He stood over six feet tall. The many years of marriage and beer drinking had carved him a splendidly remarkable gut. His stomach only added to his imposing frame. By the time I was eight or nine; his hair had turned predominantly grey, and had begun thinning. Many of his years were spent working outside or driving truck. This exposure to the sun had caused his skin to take on the appearance of soft leather. Because he was a stern authoritarian, his word was followed closely. I can't remember my mother ever having spoken back to him, with the exception of one occasion. She ended up in the hospital that day:

> In the earlier days of their marriage, my parents drank and partied rather frequently. Hard liquor did little to improve my father's disposition-quite to the contrary. He got angrier and even pushier. The one time she had opened her mouth to protest about his discipline, he had backhanded her, sending her reeling to the floor. She became highly agitated after the blow, and had to be rushed to the hospital. Her blood pressure had skyrocketed. Since that day she had been on medications for her blood pressure.

I made my way quietly towards my bedroom door. As my hand hit the doorknob, his deep voice bellowed from the living room. The sound of it startled me. Dread rushed through me like a flood.

I crossed the kitchen to the entry of the living room. My feet would not move from the kitchen floor.

I had good reason for my trepidation. I had always tried to avoid punishment at all costs. The usual method of punishment for any major infraction of the rules was a strapping. My father had been keen on hunting, and he had a hunting belt made of leather. It was approximately two inches wide and a quarter of an inch thick. The belt had leather loops on it that were designed to hold shotgun shells. One would be instructed to go to his/her room, remove their clothing, lie across the bed, and wait for the punishment to be administered.

My father spoke again. He informed me that, despite how sure I had been to the contrary, I did not have permission to leave our street to go and visit with my friend. I felt a nervous pit growing in my stomach. I knew without a doubt that this would be considered a punishable offense. He instructed me to go to my room and disrobe. Trembling from nervousness, I made my way back towards my room and shut the door behind me. I thought about my situation as I slowly began undressing and preparing for my punishment. I waited. *What was taking him so long?* The extended silence gave me time to think. I began to get a sense that something wasn't quite right. Suddenly it occurred to me why the house was so quiet. My mother and brothers were gone! I hadn't realized that the family car was not in the driveway when I climbed the hill to the house.

Suddenly much more uncomfortable, I ran naked to the window of my room, hiding behind the curtains and looking out toward the driveway. Indeed, the car was gone! I slipped back across the room and sat on my bed, nervously tugging at the covers, half covering myself. I heard him call for me from the living room-or had I? I tried to calm myself, holding my breath, listening carefully. My pulse thudding in my ears had me nearly convinced I had to be mistaken. I waited. I heard it again. Yes, it was his voice. He had called to me from the living room. I stood up, cracking the door open, listening. Again he bellowed. This time his voice indicated impatience.

I felt the breeze wafting through the kitchen as I slowly slipped into the room. Even at eight years old, I had learned about modesty. I was keenly aware that anyone looking into the windows at that moment could see my body as I slipped across the kitchen. I waited at the entry of the living room, hiding myself behind the wall that divided the kitchen from the living room. He never once looked in my direction. He merely gave instructions of what I was to do. My heart sank to the pit of my stomach. His words burned like fire into my uncomprehending brain. Confusion ruled my mind and my body refused to move. His impatience grew, and I moved merely out of fear. When he had finished giving directions, and I had followed them, I found myself in a place I did not want to be.

I looked up at the ceiling, watching the cigarette smoke swirling about as it hazed my view of the dirt and oil stained paint. The television blared at my right ear. Every so often, a soft breeze wafted through the window above my head would force the curtains high enough to block my view of the ceiling. The carpet on the floor itched madly at the skin on my back and thighs. He had me positioned at his feet, splayed out before him, my feet just inches from his. I cannot tell you about the whirlwind of feelings that tumbled through me. I trembled from fear and confusion. I wanted so desperately to run and hide. I knew this was not a thing that should happen. Everything in me told me this was wrong.

A sense of shame and violation came over me. *Why, Daddy, why?* was all I could think. I felt the desperate urge to cry, to scream out. But there was enough willfulness inside me that I would not give in. He kept me there for what seemed an eternity, looking at me as no father should look at his daughter. When he finally allowed me to get up and get dressed his one command was this: "Don't tell anyone, they'll never believe you anyway." I ran to my room ashamed and confused.

To an eight year old child, a mother and father represent the ultimate authority. At that age, a child believes that their parents know everything and possess the power to fix anything that's wrong in their world. Parents are the great protectors and nurturers of their children. That idea had not been shattered for me until that moment. So to understand where my silence in the ensuing days came from, you must remember what it is like to be eight years old. Until that moment on that warm spring day, I believed that my parents were everything. I believed they could do anything, and that they had the ability to make even the worst situations turn out well. In short, I trusted them. I believed what they said. So, in turn, I believed what he said.

My initial response was hurt confusion. I could not understand why my father would want to see any eight-year old girl's body, let alone mine. I had not even begun to develop the physical attributes of a woman. However, my father took advantage of the trust that I had placed in him. My silence fell on the situation like a blanket of consent in his twisted mind. Perhaps he'd seen it as some sort of consent, but at any rate, it opened the door for evil to prevail.

You might ask yourself why I stayed quiet. How is it that I could keep silent about something that I felt was so wrong? For one thing, my father had all the power. I believed what he said. Certainly, no one would believe me. And hadn't I broken the rules of the house? That *did* warrant punishment. Out of my own shame, and the fear of being rejected by my family, I remained silent. I feared my father's wrath more than anything else in the world. So, I walked on eggshells, trying not to break any household rules. I tried desperately not to be noticed by him. I was convinced by him that my mother would find out and that she would throw me out of the house. I cried myself to sleep night after night, wondering how I was going to be good all the time. I didn't like this new method of "punishment." I tried as hard as I could over the next days to not draw attention to myself. I stayed out of sight as much as possible. My father had broken a sacred trust. He had stolen my sense of dignity from me. What is more, he had opened a door.

Shortly after that incident, I lay in bed one night, struggling to get to sleep. I heard my father's footfalls as he crossed the kitchen towards the bathroom. The house was old, and the wood floors creaked in protest to his massive weight. I listened as he ran the water, finishing his bathroom routine, and listened as he walked back out of the bathroom. Suddenly, I heard the protestation of my doorknob as he turned it, entering my room. He lumbered across the room and sat on the edge of my bed. I froze in fear, not quite understanding why it was he had entered my room. He began talking to me. He was telling me how he knew how to make me feel good. He said that I could be his "special girl". He began to put his hands on me. I was repulsed by his touch and his beer drenched breath. I fought back the nausea that rose up from my stomach and closed my eyes tightly. My hands were clenched tightly, twisted in the sheets on the bed, pulling them tightly up around my neck. I curled my body tightly away from him; but he would not be discouraged. He reached up under the side of the bed covers, his hands clawing at my pajamas.

Somehow, he had managed to get his hands inside my pajamas. All the while he had been talking to me about how he wanted to make me feel good. How, if I would just relax, I could be his good little girl. All my struggling had been in vain.

I hadn't said anything about his new form of punishment, so I could not understand why he was coming into my room. He seemed to relish the power he had over me. His nighttime visits became quite frequent. I tried to pretend to be asleep. I suppressed my breathing and tensed my body so that it had no softness in it. I did everything I could to deter him. He would have none of it.

During those night visits, I tried hard as I could to block out as much of what was happening as possible. I learned that if I held my breath long enough, I could "change" my level of consciousness. It was almost as though he was doing what he was doing to someone else. The painful reality was that it was me he was violating. The ability to "change my consciousness" helped to block out some of the pain. After he would leave, I would lie in bed, feeling defeated and powerless, rolling my head back and forth over the pillow. I would hum myself to sleep as tears stung my eyes.

At some point, he had apparently decided that his nighttime visits were becoming too risky. He began invent reasons for my mother and brothers to leave the house without me. He had much more freedom during these times, and the level of his perversion increased with each encounter. What had satisfied him during the previous encounter would no longer be good enough in the following one. Things progressed over the coming years, to the point where he was perpetrating sodomy on a regular basis.

Perhaps the darkest moment of my childhood can help you understand how inhuman I felt. It is a moment that shaped so much of my life for so long. It was a hot summer day, sweltering, actually. Mom and the boys had once again left me alone with dad. He had already finished with me. I was lying in the bathtub, naked. His urine still moistened my hair and skin. My face was pressed against the soap scum covered porcelain as I wretched both

14

physically and emotionally, trying to get the taste of his urine from my mouth. I lay there for what seemed like forever, not having the strength to move. I felt entirely defeated. I stared up at the showerhead, the peeling paper on the walls, and the ceiling stained with mildew. Once I finally worked up enough strength to try to get up and pull myself together, I peeled my face from the porcelain and pulled up to rest my chin on the side of the tub. I glanced with disdain at the toilet that was adjacent to the tub. Its odor did nothing to help me rid myself of the acrid taste in my mouth. I stared at the toilet. I remember thinking to myself that it was what I amounted to-a toilet. I had become a waste receptacle. I slid back down into the tub and vomited. One final out-cry, and I collapsed in tears. I somehow managed to pull myself together, shower, and get dressed. But no amount of soap and water could undo what had been done.

At the age of fourteen, these encounters ceased suddenly with the onset of my monthly cycle. Apparently the possibility of getting his daughter pregnant or encountering the monthly discharge was distasteful to him. Whatever the reason for their cessation, the damage had already been done. He had broken the trust that should exist between a father and daughter. He introduced an innocent child to a sexually immoral lifestyle. He had stolen my innocence and destroyed my self-esteem.

One of the most devastating immediate side-effects of this childhood trauma was the affect it had on my relationship with my mother. Shortly after his nighttime visits had commenced, her attitude towards me began to change. She became gruff and seemed angry whenever I was in her presence. I could not understand why. I hugged her as much as I could. I tried to cheer her while trying to find some kind of comfort for myself. I felt like I was trapped between the two of them. His perverted controlling nature was far worse than her silent anger, which cut to the bone as it was. As the months rolled by, it seemed that even looking at me proved to be a difficult task for my mother. The only time she spoke to me was to instruct me on what chores needed to be done.

I was so desperate for approval. I would do extra chores, especially on the weekends, trying to please her. I wanted her to be proud of me. I brought home good grades from school. I tried to excel in everything. Each time I reached out, she would draw away angrily. Eventually, I stopped reaching out. I started to learn that the safest place for me was drawn into myself. I began spending a lot of time alone, sitting and contemplating my situation, licking my wounds. I was angry and felt sorry for myself.

To say that it was difficult to live in such a situation would be an understatement. I only wanted the situation to end. I wished that I had a different family. ANY other family would do. I could not seem to escape my father's attention, nor could I gain the attention of my mother. I only wanted her to love me. My mind reeled at her anger. *What had I done?*

My father had no realization of God's purpose for children. It has often been said that if you do not understand the purpose of a thing, you are bound to abuse it. My father did not understand at that time, or any time in his life, that I had purpose in God's ordered world--all children do. Because he did not understand the purpose of having a daughter, it was easier for my father to pervert the relationship.

The only real pleasant memories I had from my childhood were of trips to my grandparents' house. My grandfather was a wonderful man. He taught me how to waltz, carrying me on the tops of his feet as he showed me the steps. They had a large swimming pool. We would spend hours there, especially on the weekends. I can also remember the dark emotion of depression sweeping over me whenever we would leave.

Desperation flowed over me on the rides back to the house after our visits. Despair and darkness descended upon me. I sat on the door-side of the back seat, always behind my father, it seemed. I watched miles upon miles of roadside zip past my view. The areas we drove through were not vastly populated, except by a great number of trees. It actually made for a pretty show in the autumn as the leaves gave their last and fluttered to the floor of the woods. The blended colors were magnificent as they whizzed past. But it had become a rare thing that I saw the colors in those days. I could not shake the images that would force themselves into my conscious thought. My hand rested on the door handle. I leant against the door and thought to myself, *it would only take a second...it would be over...they probably wouldn't even notice.* Even that kind of sudden, painful end seemed to be better than what I was dealing with at the time. Even then, I didn't know what stopped me from pulling up on the door handle of the car door. I do know now, however, that God's hand was on my life. I know without a doubt that God kept me. While I had nearly lost my mind in the turmoil and pain that had become my life, God had kept me from insanity. I could not see the mercy in it back then. I would have done anything to make the screaming in my soul stop. But God knew, if I had been successful in ending my life, the screaming would never stop.

And so, I lived in virtual silence throughout my later teen years. I kept to myself. I had no friends of which to speak. I never dated. I didn't feel that I was worthy of having a date. I felt used, filthy, and worthless. I can remember very few things in my childhood that I would consider to be treasured memories. As my graduation from high school approached, I prepared to make my way into the world. I excelled in my Junior and Senior years of high school, because I had a goal in mind. That goal was to get out of and as far away from my parent's house as possible.

I had contacted a military recruiter and began the process of enlisting in the DEP (Delayed Entry Program). As soon as high school was finished, I could leave for the military. The paperwork was completed and signed on one precondition: I had to lose some weight. It was necessary for me to meet the height and weight standards in order to be inducted. Since my pre-teen years, I had struggled with my weight. I had never been petite or thin. I had always carried few extra pounds. Depression and pain had driven me to eating. I would come home from school and sneak snacks or pull crumbs out of the bottom of a layer cake. I was doing everything I could to fill the void. But, nothing worked; so I kept trying. I kept my silence. I bore up under the stress of being victimized and did what I had to do to get away as soon as I could.

The recruiter that I had been working with generously offered to come and run with me in the evenings. He had even brought a sauna suit in which I could run. It seemed that he was as enthused as I was about my entry into the military. On the second or third occasion that he showed up to run with me, things took a strange turn. We ran down our usual path. The sun filtered in through the trees. The summer heat had me sweating in no time. Without warning, he suddenly stopped. He took me by the hand, pulling me into the foliage that lined the roadside as I dragged my feet trying to pull away from him. He trapped me in a wooded area and took advantage of the privacy a stone wall provided.

It appeared that I had "victim" stamped on my forehead now. This was not the only incident of someone exercising such power over me. My father was only the first. In most every situation, I felt I had no choice. I had often wondered if he had "sold me up the river" or told these people about what they could get out of me. Tolerating this situation was my way out of the hell in which I had been living for so many years. And so, again, I kept the pain inside. I tolerated his unwanted advances so that I could escape.

Chapter 2

Seeds Produce Fruit After Their Own Kind.

My father had started me out on my walk in powerlessness. He had stolen my innocence and perverted my desire for approval. The things he had done to me for so very long violated me in ways that cannot be understood by most. He had managed to make me feel less than human. While it might not be fathomable to some why I kept silent throughout my teen years, why I did not cry out in desperation, one might ask why I tolerated such treatment from others. I had thought endlessly about asking for help as a child. I thought about going to see the counselors in our local high school, of telling one of my very few friends, and of running away. But where was there to go? Who could I tell? And there in the balance of all those thoughts was the voice of my father lingering in my mind. "If the family breaks up, everyone will blame you. No one will believe you". I thought so much about committing suicide, just ending it all. I was screaming on the inside, yet no one heard. I just wanted the pain to stop. But there was also the consideration of appearances. It was crucial to my father that everything appeared as normal as possible to those on the outside. It infuriated him for anyone to come poking around the family and asking questions. It completely maddened him to lose control.

Psychologically, it is fairly simple to explain. I had been gradually indoctrinated and had become accustomed to being treated in such a manner. I didn't know anything else. In the simplest of terms, you could say I was brainwashed. My father always told me that it was the thing that made him happy. My father also told me that if I ever told anyone what "we" did in private, he would deny it. He told me that all the girls did this for their daddies. Perhaps the biggest card he played was what such an exposure would do to the family. It would surely tear the family apart. Everyone would blame the failure of the family on me. I would be hated and despised for the rest of my life. I heard this over and over again, on almost a daily basis. Garbage in-garbage out. If you plant tomato seeds, do you not get tomatoes? My father would reap exactly what he had sown. Unfortunately, for a very long while, I would be the one who suffered under the memory of what my father had done.

On August 26, 1980, a scant six weeks after graduating from high school, I departed for basic training. I was flown to Fort McClellan, Alabama. I spent my eighteenth birthday in the barracks that would be my home for the next two months. The training cycle was not due to start until two days later.

I embraced military training. Within it lay the discipline and personal challenge that seemed right for me at that time. I made every effort to excel in everything I did. Upon completion of basic training, I went on to AIT (Advanced Individual Training). That cycle of specialized training lasted approximately twelve weeks. Stationed at Fort Gordon, Georgia, I underwent training to become a tactical communications specialist. It was an odd area of work for me to choose. I did not have the foresight at that time to think about what I wanted to do with the rest of my life. When I signed up for the military, my only goal was to get out of my parent's house. I didn't look where I was going. I took the first occupational specialty they suggested that I would do well in, in accordance with my ASVAB (Armed Services Vocational Aptitude Battery) scores.

After about two weeks of training, we were given out first weekend pass. We had seventy-two hours to do whatever it was we wanted to do, as long as we did not leave the military base. Some of the other females from my barracks went over to the bowling alley to play a few games. I followed along, preferring such an activity to staying cooped up in my room. I had never bowled before in my life. The bowling alley was dimly lit. It smelled of scorched cheese, beer, and sweaty shoes. We rented shoes, picked out balls, and tried to have some fun. I bowled terribly. I can still remember my score-55. But, bowling was not the only thing I did for the first time that night. I had consumed a few beers. By the time we were halfway into our second game

I was feeling no pain. For the first time in a very long time, I felt happy. The alcohol had helped me to forget about all I had been through. I liked the feeling. The forgetting was wonderful.

My inebriation caused me to over-exaggerate everything I did. This caused me to catch the attention of one of the permanently stationed males. He sat back and watched as we played poorly and laughed. He seemed amused with us, and once I realized I had caught his attention, I played up to him. We drank and joked around till nearly midnight, and then stumbled back to our barracks.

The next morning, we went to the mess hall (cafeteria), to eat breakfast. On the weekends, the alternate mess hall was used. As we made our way through the line, my jaw nearly hit the floor. There he stood, behind the serving line, grinning from ear to ear. It was the same guy from the night before! Aside from having a pounding headache from a hangover and wishing everyone would whisper, now I also had to deal with the embarrassment. The other females teased me mercilessly.

I learned that he was a cook, permanently stationed at Fort Gordon. I was only there for a short time. I saw no harm in spending a bit of time with him. Jimmy and I had become acquainted and started seeing each other. The relationship went beyond the boundaries of military regulation. Trainees were not allowed to date permanently stationed personnel. That was made abundantly clear to all trainees. However, that didn't seem to matter to him, and so, likewise, it did not matter to me. He had cash, a car, and showed me attention. That was good enough reason for me to spend time with him. After a couple of weeks of dating, he had broached the subject of becoming physical with one another. The suggestion had taken me by surprise, and I was not quite sure what to do. He suggested that things would be safe. I had been on contraceptives since basic training. The doctors there had prescribed them to enable my body to become better regulated. Yet, in my mind, it was a huge step.

We conquered the logistical issues of getting together all too quickly for my liking. He told me he would sneak me into his barracks room during the weekend. He would arrange for us to have privacy. It was the first time in my life that I would willingly give my body to another. I wish I could say it was some wonderful, life changing experience, but it was not. It was not even something I wanted to do. It was simply what someone else expected. There I went again, trying to make others happy.

We continued seeing each other throughout my training cycle. My platoon sergeant caught wind of the relationship, but he'd never said a word about it. It appeared that I had garnered favor from him through my performance as a trainee. I kept my room spotless, my uniform was always impeccable, and I always followed through with instructions. So while the other females were stuck in rooms with three or four trainees, I had my own room. While the other females were stuck in the barracks for a GI party (clean-up), I was allowed to roam about as I pleased.

Jimmy and I had taken several short trips in the area around the base as my training cycle neared an end.

Our last trip was to be a major one, to Aiken, South Carolina. Just before the trip, he met me after last formation that Friday. As we sat in his car talking, he took a small box from his pocket. He asked me to marry him. I contemplated his proposal cautiously. I weighed the options. It was the first time that anyone had ever taken a genuine interest in me. Someone finally wanted me! But somehow, I wasn't quite sure that I felt the same way.

I had begun to get leery. The things that I once thought were cute and endearing had begun to worry me. He would always be lurking around. When I showed up for first formation, he was there. At the closing formation at the end of the day, he was there. He would tap his watch in a gesture which meant to hurry. I would go up to my room and change my clothes, hurrying down so we could leave together. It seemed I didn't have any friends other than the ones with whom he spent time. I used to think that all of this constant attention was cute. But by the end of the training cycle, it had become unnerving.

But I had become infatuated with the idea of being a married woman. I liked the idea that someone was interested in me. But to say that I truly loved this man would have been an exaggeration. Despite all my reservations, I accepted his proposal. We were supposed to wed in Aiken that following weekend. But, some sort of technicality kept the ceremony from taking place. Before I left to return home, he gave me the box that had our wedding bands in it. When I finished my eight week tour as a recruiter's aide, and went on to Europe, he would meet me there. He gave me the name of a soldier to go and see about getting his orders diverted so that we could be together.

I met with the young man to which Jimmy had referred me. He was in personnel, and would be able to help Jimmy get orders in the same area. Ronnie and I hit it off almost immediately. We began seeing each other. I wrote my former betrothed a "Dear John" letter and pushed him far back in my memory. I didn't give much thought to how he would feel or what he might do. I only knew the sense of freedom was exciting.

Ronnie and I were nearly inseparable for about a year. I fell head over heels in love with him so quickly. It was four months into the relationship when I discovered that he was married. I was so hurt to learn that he had lied to me. But, he made sense out of the situation for me. I suppose in my heart, I wanted it to make sense. His wife was all the way back in the United States. What harm was I doing anyone? I bought it. I bought it because I wanted to. He had a charismatic personality. He was in charge of the personnel issues for his unit, and he also moonlighted at a local nightclub in town. He was quite popular with the ladies. I enjoyed being the one who was special enough to have his undivided attention.

We spent a great deal of time together. We went to festivals on the economy. We would kick back and listen to music in his barracks room. I had even developed quite a skill for frying chicken, which made me a hit throughout the barracks building.

It came time for Ronnie to leave and return to the states. When he did leave, I became deeply depressed and felt lost. He had arranged for a friend of his to "look after me." At the time, I thought it was a sweet gesture of concern. In hindsight, I knew that he had given the "replacement" the 411 about me. The torch had been passed.

This "replacement" and I hung out and listened to music in my studio apartment. Female barracks were in short supply; so when I was offered the opportunity to live on the economy, I jumped. My small efficiency apartment afforded me a great deal of privacy. Ronnie's replacement had a great deal less time to spend with me than Ronnie had. I began to find things to do to keep myself busy. I would go to the clubs on post and off post. It really didn't matter what kind of club it was. If there was alcohol there, I would close the club down. I would stagger home highly intoxicated. Sometimes I was alone, other times not. Although a good number of visitors passed through my apartment, none could have been called a significant relationship. I simply did not want to be alone and sober. If I had to be alone, I wanted to be drunk.

I had been introduced to hashish when I had been hanging with Ronnie and his roommates. The deeper my depression tried to cut, the more I smoked and drank. Countless times, I would awaken, choking in my own vomit. The pain that I had tried to run away from ate at my core. The spirits that had been transferred onto me by my father and my other perpetrators were still with me, and they were manifesting in my behavior. As much as I tried avoiding feeling anything at all, the feelings continued to rush into my conscious mind. I loathed how I felt and tried to drown it out. I searched desperately for love and kindness. Every single one of those one-night-stands was a new hope for a relationship-or so I thought. In my twisted perception, giving in to the sexual demands of others was how I gained acceptance and approval. In that search for approval, I learned I would do anything it took. My desire for acceptance and love lead to every manner of depravity.

I began to despise who I had become. I didn't want to let anyone in. I had been hurt so many times that I didn't want to be hurt again. I built walls around me, because I needed to keep others out. Rejecting them out of hand was so much easier for me than dealing with their rejection once they came to know me. I became pushy and boorish. I started doing drugs on a regular basis when the alcohol would no longer make me forget. 1 Corinthians 6:16 (NIV) says "Do you not know that he who unites himself with a prostitute is one with her in body? For it is said, 'The two will become one flesh'." This does not only apply to the prostitute, but anyone with whom you have an intimate relationship. The two become one. There is a spiritual exchange that takes place.

I had become one with so many that I had no idea who I was any longer. It all went back to my relationship with my father. That relationship was the catalyst. The spirit that dwelt within me because of our relationship was so powerful that I was helpless to stop it. I did not understand the nature of spiritual things. I simply believed I was just not a good person. It would be many years before I would learn that the contrary was true.

Chapter Three

Band-aid Therapy For A Compound fracture

In August of 1982, I returned to the continental United States and was stationed at Fort Hood, Texas. It was a new beginning. I had determined that this time things would be different. I had grown exhausted from my search for something to fill the vacuum in my life. I began to think about having children and what I would do for the rest of my life. If I could not find a man to love me, certainly a child would do. A child would love me! In September, I met Sammy. He was a bright spot in my day. He told me he had watched me for days before he had approached me. His barracks were adjacent to mine. He had monitored my comings and goings, and had developed an interest in me. We began dating. We would go to one of the clubs on post and drink and party with friends. We spent time walking and talking. Soon, Sammy filled all my spare hours.

A quick three months after our first date, we decided to get married. We called his parents on

Thanksgiving weekend to tell them the good news. Things weren't perfect—far from it. Sam liked to drink. But I figured I could control things in that respect. We began looking for a place where we could live after we got married. Between Thanksgiving and Christmas, things took an ugly turn. Sammy was in the field with his unit on a field exercise. Reportedly, he had been drinking while in the field. He then proceeded to get behind the wheel of a military vehicle. Admittedly, it was a bad set of decisions, both infractions of military regulations. A date was set for his Article 15 (court) hearing. Such a hearing is convened to listen to the evidence concerning the case and for judgement to be passed.

With his Article 15 pending, Sammy became somber and angry. After hearing of the incident, my company commander called me into his office. He questioned me about my plans for the future. Although it was strict policy for commanders not to interfere in the personal lives of their soldiers, he seemed to feel the need. He had told me that if I married Sammy, my life would go nowhere because

Sammy was going nowhere. He told me that Sammy's military career would be cut short because of such an unfortunate incident. I could not see the logic in what he said; I had accounted his interference as bigotry because Sammy was African-American. Prejudice was still very prevalent in those years, especially in the south.

Despite the obstacles, we married on January 7, 1983. Very shortly afterward, Sammy was given a less than honorable discharge from the military. I was still serving the remainder of my enlistment. My being the bread-winner in the household caused Sammy to become moody and agitated. The longer he looked (or didn't look) for a job, the more he would brood over his lack of success. He began to drink heavily, attending every party in the community. He had also hosted his fair share of parties. The red flags that I refused to see before marrying him became abundantly clear as time progressed.

In August of 1983, I opted out of re-enlistment. By September we had left the Fort Hood area to settle in El Paso, Texas. Neither of us had a job, or any money. His parents had agreed to provide us with a place to stay until we became gainfully employed. Surprisingly, that happened relatively quickly for both of us. Sammy had found employment with a security firm after he completed a security guard course. I found work with a convenience store chain. Soon, we had an apartment on the west side of town. Things seemed to be moving along rather well. Sammy's disposition even improved, although his drinking habits hadn't.

In March of 1985, much to my pleasure, I had discovered I had become pregnant. I worked up until about the seventh month, and then stayed home to complete the pregnancy. As time went by, money got tighter. But I didn't let that bother me because I had a special contentment--a new hope. Leketia Marie was born on December 5, 1985. Sitting in the hospital room, recovering from a cesarean section delivery, I was struggling to deal with the pain. The nurse came in around 11:00 in the morning, wheeling the baby into the room in a clear bassinette. The nurse laid Leketia in my arms.

As I held her for the first time, I looked down on her with wonder. My heart swelled with joy. *Finally, I had someone who would love me!* I gently stroked her face, speaking sweetly to her. I checked for ten fingers and ten toes. I put her to breast. She was everything for which I had hoped.

My elation was short lived. I nursed her through the six-week recovery period. Breast-feeding makes birth control pills an unacceptable option. I was advised to abstain from intimate contact for at least as long as I would be nursing. Incredibly, I learned at my post-natal check-up at eight weeks that I was once again pregnant. Sam had refused to abstain, and had also adamantly refused to use any sort of contraception. Although I was shocked about the pregnancy, I did my best to adjust to the idea of another new arrival.

In April, I went for a routine visit, only to learn days later that the Pap smear had indicated degenerative changes in the tissue of the cervix. Subsequently I learned that the baby had died at the end of the first trimester. I was advised that I could go home and simply wait for my body to expel the "tissue", or I could have a D & C. I elected to have the procedure done. The doctor had intimated it would be more convenient for him, and it would be less painful for me.

Admittedly, the physical pain may have been less, but the procedure left me feeling as though the life had been sucked out of me, literally. When Sam brought me home from the surgical center, he left me alone. Apparently, dealing with the pain of a lost child was too much for him. He went off with his brother to drown his sorrows. I was left to take care of my infant daughter in the midst of a suffocating void.

Things began to look up as Sam snagged a coveted position with Southern Pacific Railroad shortly after Leketia was born. The labor was hard and the hours were long. The "gangs" as they were called, would sometimes work in areas outside of the city. Being a track laborer was hard on the body. Soon, it began to take a toll on Sam's knee. He had suffered an injury to the knee in a rock-climbing fall while in the military. The VA doctors had advised him that he had torn his anterior cruciate ligament almost entirely away from the cartilage. They planned a reconstructive surgery.

The surgery went smoothly and the doctors said that, for the time being, he would be fine. At some point farther down the road, they had said, he would either have to have wires placed in his leg, forcing his knee permanently straight, or have the lower portion of his leg amputated. His recovery went well, although he brooded over having to use the brace the doctors had prescribed. Against his doctor's advice, he drank alcohol while on pain medications.

He could not return to labor with the railroad until the doctors had given him clearance. He took work again with a security company to keep money coming in. He refused to let me work, stating I should be home taking care of Leketia. And while we were at it, why not have another baby? I shuddered at the thought and continued to take birth control pills. His security job was not bringing in the kind of money his railroad job had been. His disability payments from the VA were taking forever to process. We began to fall behind on rent payments. We robbed Peter to pay Paul. Sam hated that situation. He wanted to be able to support his family. I tried to get him to apply for government assistance such as food stamps, but he refused. As head of the household, he had to be the one to apply. This left me with some difficult decisions. Do I buy diapers for the baby, or do I get my birth control pills refilled? There really wasn't enough money to do all that was needed.

I had to let my prescription run out, and hoped that I would not come up pregnant again. However, in May of 1987, I discovered that I was indeed pregnant again. At first I was angry. I was angry about my situation, about his stubbornness, and about the pregnancy. As time went on, I gradually warmed to the idea of having another baby. When I felt the baby move, I actually became happy about it.

The financial stress got to be too much for Sam. He began to drink even more. He had taken to going on all night drinking binges with his brother. It didn't seem to matter to him that the money for alcohol wasn't there. For him, it seemed that beer came before bread on his list of priorities. One morning, when I was about seven months pregnant, I awoke to the sound of the key in the door. I had become accustomed to his early morning returns, and had developed a practice of pretending to be sound asleep. I would continue to act as though I were dead asleep, avoiding his attention, until he would pass out.

On this particular morning, he stumbled in the door at around 7:00a.m. He began bellowing and screaming at me. Everything was wrong with his life, and when he was intoxicated, it was always my fault. He began asking me who I had been sleeping with me in his bed while he was out. The alcohol made him angry; and he lacked self-control when he was drunk. He backed me against a wall, the baby in my arms. As he yelled and screamed at me, I slid down the wall until I was sitting on the floor. He began swinging at me, screaming that I was a whore. I hoped that one of the neighbors would hear the noise and call the police. The police were never called.

When he had exhausted himself of his tirade, he lay down on the couch and passed out. I covered him with a blanket and went to get cleaned up. When he left for work later that day, I got dressed and got the baby ready to go. I walked over to the apartment complex manager's office and asked to use the phone (ours had been disconnected). I called the police and filed a report. When the police came, I told them I wanted to leave. They took me to the battered women's shelter.

While I stayed there, I made several phone calls to Sammy trying to negotiate my return to our residence. I would not come back, I had told him, unless he got help for his drinking problem. He refused to admit to having a problem. The precondition of my return to the home being therapy, he agreed to go. Going served little purpose, however; because Sam refused to admit he

46

had a problem, and participated in the therapy as little as possible. But he did agree to the therapy, so I had already returned home.

At about thirty-seven weeks into the pregnancy, the doctor performed an ultrasound examination. He reported that the baby would be a boy and would weigh about eight pounds. I don't think anyone was more surprised when Samantha Nicole was born than her father. He waited at the hospital until I came out of the anesthesia to tell me that the baby was a girl. I can tell you that the look on his face was not one of a happy new father. He left the hospital and didn't come back until it was time for me to leave to go home. He cited work as his reason, but I knew he hadn't been working more than eight hours a day, if that much.

When I arrived home from the hospital, Leketia was filthy; her hair had not been brushed, and she was still in her pajamas. I cannot truly be sure what had taken place while I was in the hospital recuperating from the delivery; and part of me doesn't really want to know. Things could not have been much worse. Yet, I continued to work at making the marriage work. I was determined for the marriage not to be yet another failure in my life.

Please understand that I was not perfectly innocent in the marriage. I did plenty to provoke his anger. We were both immature. I knew that he hated to have his father lecture him about anything. As things got worse in the marriage, I would call his father and update him on his son's latest wrong-doings. I would then sit and giggle quietly as he had to endure endless phone lectures about his behavior. I did nothing, however, to deserve his physical and emotional abuse.

Sam finally got called back to work with the railroad. This time there was a complication; the job site was far from home. He had asked me to leave El Paso to go with him. He proposed that we could live in one of the trailers that the railroad provided for families. We would follow the "gang" as it worked the line. Somehow, this plan didn't seem like the stable life that I wanted for my girls. I wanted them to have a good home, childhood friends, and a lot of pleasant memories. I opted to stay in El Paso while Sam went out of town during the week and came home on weekends. Soon, his returns home became as infrequent as once every three weeks. He claimed he was working overtime and could seldom find the opportunity to come home.

Sam was bitter over my decision not to travel with him. It had begun to seem abundantly clear that we did not have the same agendas. We were not working toward the same goal in the same way. And I can admit that my decision might not have seemed fair to him, but I had to do what was best for the children. He would call on weekends, apparently intoxicated, and say the cruelest things. The next day he would call again and begin talking to me as though nothing had happened. He would be so intoxicated during some of his phone calls, he would never remember them. My life became an emotional roller coaster. One day I was the best thing that happened to him, the next day I was a whore who was cheating on him and sucking his wallet dry.

Although he claimed to have been working so much overtime, all he ever could manage to send home for the children and me would be about $300 every two weeks. This was far short of the money we needed to meet the rent and feed the children. With him gone so much of the time, I was left to fend off the bill collectors by myself. We had again fallen behind on our rent and I had had enough. I decided that I would go out and get a job, despite the fact that it would anger him. We needed the money.

I got a job at a Mexican food restaurant. The supervisor was willing to let me work differing shifts to enable me to pay less in day care. Sam was very angry when he learned I had gotten a job. He began insinuating that I only wanted a job so that I could meet other people and find someone else with whom to sleep. I worked as many hours as they would let me. When I came home, I had to take care of the children and the house. Even if I had had the desire to find someone else to sleep with, I certainly didn't have the energy or the time.

He continued to leave to work out of town with the railroad gang, returning about one weekend every three weeks or so. On November 8, 1989, my life changed drastically. He called that evening, apparently intoxicated. He went on and on about how miserable I was as a wife. He told me that he had found a girl and that they were dating. He said they were in love. I was crushed. I felt as though my heart had sunk to my feet. I refused to believe him. I told him that he would call the next morning not even remembering what he had said that night. He told me that he would call me the next day and tell me once again so I would know he meant it. He called me the following day, though, his story had changed slightly. He told me that he had only seen the girl once. He promised he would not see her again. For some reason, I tended to believe that the previous night's version held more truth.

I told him to give me some space. I needed time to sort out what had just taken place. I began to understand some things. All of his accusations about my own infidelity were based on **his** guilt about his own. This girl, whoever she was, hadn't been the first one. That much I was certain about. She had called me and as we began to talk, we learned we had both had a similar suspicious infection at the same time. It was all I needed to know. I had made a decision that, for my own emotional and mental well being, as well as the welfare of my children, I had to divorce him.

This was a major decision, to say the least. I had no money of which to speak. Everything I made from my job went to the kids and the bills. A divorce was expensive; and I needed a lawyer. I thought to ask my parents for help. I explained the situation to them. This was a difficult task, as they grew up believing that marriage is forever. That particular value was passed down to us children. At any rate, they agreed to help me rather than watch me continue living in misery.

After the necessary paperwork was filed, Sam came back that December to see the girls and to sign the papers. He did not plan to contest the divorce, and had even agreed to pay a generous amount in child support. The night before the meeting with my lawyer to sign the papers, he came to my apartment. As I cooked dinner for the girls, he sat on the kitchen counter asking for another chance. He asked me not to go through with the divorce. It would hurt the girls, he had said. His voice became more plaintive as I paid little attention to him. He had told me it was over with the other girl, that he would never see her again. Pleading with me, tears streaming down his cheeks, he almost seemed sincere. Yet something deep inside began speaking to me. The longer he spoke, the louder the voice from within became. I began to hear it very clearly speaking to me. *"Don't trust him. He's lying. He'll do it again if you give him another chance"*. At the time I did not understand from where the voice had come or why. I only know that heeding the voice was the wisest choice. I denied him a second chance and sent him on his way. I learned a couple months later that just two days before he sat on the counter crying and pleading for another chance, he had put the girl up in an apartment.

Chapter Four

Breaking Generational Curses

The final divorce hearing was scheduled with the court. On Tuesday, January 21st, I went before the magistrate to sign the paperwork and finalize the arrangements. I was nearly free. I was so elated that I decided to go out and celebrate. I went to one of the local dance clubs to drink, relax, and dance. I arrived early and sat at a table at the end of the dance floor, across from the entrance. I watched as others arrived. At the other end of the dance floor, I noticed a man sitting at another table. It seemed peculiar to me that he was reading a book in the darkness of the club.

I finished my first glass of wine, and ordered a second, trying to work up the nerve to ask him to dance. He was a fine looking man, military haircut, and had a nice physique. But the book....yes the book did hit me strangely. He rose from his chair and moved towards the door. I gasped, *No, no, please don't go*! I thought. A moment or two later he had returned and sat back down. He had only gone to hang up his coat. I sighed in relief and decided that it was time to make my move.

I learned that he was in the military, and was not a bad dancer at all. He had just recently been stationed at Fort Bliss. So recently, in fact, that he did not even have a car yet. I learned the book he was reading was called Shakespeare's "The Tempest". We danced and talked well into the night. I have a tendency to use my hands a lot when I talk. I know I made a big impression on him; because while talking, I knocked his coke out of his hand. The glass crashed to the floor, breaking into pieces and spilling his drink. I found myself drawn to him. There was something decidedly different about him. Something told me not to let this one get away.

I explained to him about my divorce, and how it was to be finalized the day after next. I asked if he would like to go out on a date and help me celebrate my new found freedom and he agreed. On January 23, 1990, my divorce from Sam was finalized, and I had my first date with Charles. We dated steadily, talking on the phone until all hours when we could not be together. In May of that year, we moved in with each other. On February 14, 1991, we wed at a local office of the Justice of the Peace.

Charles was by far the best thing that had happened to me in all my days. He was generous, caring, and intelligent. He allowed me freedom I had never had before. He doted on me. He accepted my girls as his own right from the very beginning. It was like living in heaven. I didn't have to work if I didn't want to. It was in the midst of such happiness that I had to deal with my mother suffering and dying from cancer.

That November found my mother laying on her deathbed. Bone cancer had eaten through the vertebrae in her spine, partially paralyzing her. From her appearance, it was in more than just her bones. I had received a call from my father about her condition, and went home, at mother's behest. She wanted her family around her.

The night following my arrival, I had taken a break from the bedside vigil over my mother to get some sleep. The call came the next morning that she was in a coma. My younger brother and his wife came out to my father's house. Amidst the chaos, she and I decided to take a walk. In a conversation with my sister-in-law that morning, I learned that my mother had known what my father had been doing all those years. It was no wonder she had grown angry and bitter. What was surprising was that it was then that I learned that my younger brother had walked in on an encounter between my father and me.

Apparently, the pain of what he had seen had become too much for him. He took to drinking to numb the pain. He had been doing better in recent days, she had said, but worried how my mother's passing might affect him. He had been seeing a counselor, trying to help him deal with the issues that he was experiencing. For the life of me, I could not understand why he had been so messed up by the situation. After all, I was the victim. But she told me what he had seen:

One night, I was washing dishes after dinner, and my father had begun to fondle me. My father had gotten careless in his pursuits, and it was then that my brother walked in. I had no recollection of his walking in on the situation. He had evidently seen my father with his hands inside my shirt. Hurt and shocked, he retreated from the house. He had kept the secret to himself.

Upon hearing the news, all I could think of was getting back to my mother and forgiving her for her anger. I suddenly understood that she did not know how to process the feelings she had. I wanted so much to make peace with her. My older brother had led her to the Lord before I had arrived home. I needed to make peace with her before she passed on.

After hearing these new revelations, I returned to the hospital. I paced the hospital room and the adjacent hallways, worrying, wondering if she would come back to consciousness. I watched and waited. I openly made note of her condition. A blue pallor was appearing on her toes and feet. My father chastised me for speaking about her condition while in the room. He protested that she could hear me. He believed that my comments about her condition would cause her to lose hope. He stood inches from me, shaking his finger in my face, scolding me as if I were still a small child. Between the pain of my new revelations, the impending passing of my mother, and the entire family witnessing the encounter, it got to be too much. So many years of anger and hurt came pouring out of me. I berated him. How could he feel he still had the right to talk to me as though I were a young child? I was not a child.

I wanted to talk at that very moment about the pain that he caused all of us; and about how messed up the family had become. I wanted to confront him with the pain he had caused me. When I opened my mouth to speak, I was once again chastised. I was told that it was not the time. The fact of the matter was, in regards to dealing with my situation as it was; there was never a good time. But I was tired of carrying it all on my own. It was at that point that my older brother pulled me out of the room and tried to counsel me. I understand now, what he was trying to say then, as I was standing in front of the hallway window. I looked out at the brown grass and naked trees, and felt the chill from the outside run through me. Pain and betrayal were all I knew or could feel. I began to wonder, when would it be my time?

Mom came around to consciousness again. This was probably the first time that I could recall her smiling when she saw me. I had the opportunity to forgive her for all the things that had happened in the past. She had made peace with God, and the world, and could then let go of the world.

The whole experience had opened anew the scars from the past. I didn't know how to process any of what had happened. I didn't know how to deal with how I felt. I had a wonderful new husband to go home to; and yet, I got little solace from that. How could I tell him about all of those things that I had experienced in my past? I know what you must be thinking. Perhaps your thoughts would be, how could I have kept it from him? But, I didn't want him to see me as damaged goods. He had already done so much to change my life for the better, how could I burden him with these old problems? Besides, I had been functioning well enough before the funeral, and I didn't want his image of me to change.

So, I bundled up all the pain and anguish and brought them back home with me. At some point, I suppose my mind had rationalized some of the things that began to happen. I began to justify some of the things I began to do as a result of how I felt after my trip home. I started going out to the dance clubs at night. I began drinking again. It was the way that I dealt with the newly exposed wounds that were screaming once again. I hated it. I had learned to hate myself, what I had become, and how I felt. My self-destructive vent progressed until I had an affair. No sooner had I entered the affair, I found myself desiring so much to leave it. I knew it would hurt Charles to know such a thing was happening. But yet again, the attention I got from the affair fed some kind of need. It quieted the screaming to some degree.

I didn't know how to process what I felt. I couldn't deal with the issues I had with the people that had caused them. That much was clear. But how could I dump such things on someone like a relatively new husband? What kind of damaged goods would he think that he had married if I told him the ugly truth about my past? I had learned, over time and repetition of historical events, that everyone I loved eventually hurt me. Charles was good. If he knew what kind of a person I was as a child and young adult, I was sure he would leave me.

As much as I needed Charles to be in my life, I needed the alcohol more to numb the pain. I had begun to hate what I was doing to Charles, and to our marriage. Subconsciously, I suppose part of me truly wanted to get caught. I wanted the affair to be over.

Eventually, Charles found one of the notes I had typed for the other man. I came home from work that day to find the house completely quiet. Calling out for him, I got no response. I went down the hallway to our bedroom. On the bed was the letter, face down. On the back of the letter he had written *"Thanks for the lesson in trust"*. I walked down and opened the girl's room. They were quietly playing on the floor. I tried the door to his office. It was locked. I knocked desperately, but he would not answer. After the kids had gone to bed that night, we had a very heated discussion. His pain was evident. I couldn't believe what I had done. I had torn his heart into pieces simply because I could not trust; because I had jammed all the negative energy deep inside me.

At that point I had sunk so low that not even the thought of being around to raise my girls was enough to make me want to continue to live. I had hit absolute rock bottom. I no longer wanted to live. I could not stop the pain. No matter what I did, I could not stop the pain nor fill the void. I remembered the plethora of medications in the bathroom medicine cabinet. I went into the bathroom and began pulling bottles down out of it. There were so many pills. I could take them all, I had surmised, and simply fade away into darkness. The darkness would be cool, quiet, and I would no longer feel any pain. I closed the door to the bathroom and began surveying the bottles, trying to figure which pills would work the quickest. As I began opening the bottles, Charles knocked on the door. He asked what I was doing. I didn't tell him. I told him "Nothing." I suppose that he had sensed that something was desperately wrong. He went to open the door to the bathroom. When I blocked the door, he became more forceful. When he saw the pills, he became even more insistent about getting the door open. We fought over the door, pushing it back and forth. I was trying to push him out and he was trying to push his way in. I remember him telling me, *"You're not gonna do this, I'm not gonna let you"*. He won the struggle over the door and quickly disposed of the pills as I sunk to the floor of the bathroom in desperation.

Our financial situation had not been the best at that time. I was working two jobs and he had just been discharged from the military. He had been searching for work, and there was very little money at the time. There was no money for a hotel room, a bus or a train ticket. There was not even enough for a tank of gas. He literally had nowhere to go or any way to get there. We were faced with existing together. Neither of us could run. I suppose God had arranged things to be just that way.

The night following my suicide attempt, we had an in-depth discussion. I laid everything out for him. I told him about my childhood experiences, and how it had affected my life up to this point. And I had to take responsibility for the decisions I had made. The trip home and my mother's death had just made all the old pain fresh and new again. I wept; he held me. During a break, we went outside for some fresh air. Standing in the night air, I looked up at the stars in the sky as I wondered aloud. I wondered how God, if He did exist, could let such a thing happen to a young girl who had never done anything to hurt anyone. *"How could He (God) do this to me?"* I asked. Just as calm as he could be, Charles simply replied, *"He didn't do it to you, He saw you through it."* It was rather a cathartic experience for me. For the first time I thought that God might actually exist, and that He might actually know that I exist.

During the course of our reconciliation, we had conceived a baby. Things slowly began to get better from there. Our son, Malcolm Alexander, was born on February 28. 1994. The pregnancy was troubled, and he was born by cesarean section. He was small, but he was perfect. When Malcolm was five months old, a friend of mine from work invited us to church. Our lives have not been the same since we set foot in Christian Joy Center. On Father's day of that year, I gave my heart to the Lord, and my husband rededicated his life. It was then that I learned that my life-saving angel was an ordained minister.

Chapter Five

Breaking up Fallow Ground

*"For in the day of trouble, He will keep me safe in
His dwelling, He will hide me in the shelter of His
tabernacle and set me upon a high rock. Then my
head will be exalted above the enemies who
surround me; at His tabernacle will I sacrifice with
shouts of joy; I will sing and make music to the
Lord."* Psalms 27:5-6 (NIV)

The ministry was nothing like I had ever
experienced before. The music was lively; the
songs based on scripture. There was nothing typical
about it for me. I noticed people from just about
every ethnic group in attendance. I enjoyed the
music. It was like nothing I had ever heard in
church before. I learned through this "teaching"
ministry, that becoming born again was merely the
first step in a long walk.

The first few services proved to be a challenge for
me. I had a hard time reconciling my experiences

with the "given" fact that God was a true and loving Father. I had suffered so much. I had become so bitter that I viewed the ministry and those in it with some skepticism at first. Nonetheless, I listened intently to the Pastor week after week. He preached that there was a plan for our lives, that God had our best interests at heart; and that He loves us. The thought that kept turning up in my mind was *"How could anyone love me the way I am?" "How could there be a plan for **me**?"* I had felt for so many years that I had been tossed to and fro on a violent sea of trouble. There was a plan in this? Perhaps the only thing that kept me at the church was hope that it was true.

On that fateful Father's day, an alter call had commenced. Because I had been raised up in the Catholic Church, the concept was foreign to me. I had never seen such a thing. People rose from their seats, tears streaming from their eyes. Standing with the congregation, I was taken aback and bewildered. One of the ministers had approached and took my hand to lead me forward. A turning point had come in my life. I stood at the altar, shoulder to shoulder with the others. As the Pastor made his way down the line, I felt something stir from within me. When he approached me, the Pastor led me in the prayer for salvation, the prayer of repentance. In one quick moment, every sin I had ever committed was erased. I now had a friend upon whom I could rely. His name was Jesus. Someone cared for me!

The initial excitement of this new journey I had begun quickly waned. The feelings of guilt and shame managed to bring themselves to the forefront of my mind nearly daily, which lead to my reactionary behavior. This type of behavior would be considered unacceptable, even to those who are not born again. But I did my best to keep my emotions in check.

In the weeks and months that followed, my knowledge of the scriptures began to increase. The only scripture I had known prior to arriving at the ministry was John 3:16. This was not because I had ever opened a bible, but because you always saw some "holy roller" flashing it on a big piece of cardboard at football games. My brother had sent me a bible when he became born again. John 3:16 was the only scripture I had looked up in the bible before I placed it on a shelf to collect dust.

The more I learned, the more I began to hear a voice that questioned whether it was all true. The enemy will often come and try to reclaim what he views is his. Again, I was faced with doubt. I had begun to think that indeed God had sent His son. However, the sad fact was that I had a hard time believing that He had sent His son for *me*. I never really felt that I was worth such a sacrifice.

For months I continued to go to church. My husband and I found a place to work within the ministry. Working in children's church was beneficial to me at the time. There were no structured lesson plans; and we had to research the scriptures ourselves and build a lesson plan around whatever point was set out for the children that week. We continued to attend week after week. I had noticed that people would sometimes stand up during prayer and begin to speak in other languages.

This manner of speech was often accompanied by excitement and tears. After inquiring, I learned that these people were using their spiritual language.

I decided that I wanted to have such a language for myself. I wanted the power that a prayer language could give me. I wanted a direct unhindered "phone line" to God. "In the same way, the Spirit helps us in our weakness. We do not know what we ought to pray for, but the Spirit Himself intercedes for us with groans that words cannot express. And he who searches our hearts knows the mind of the Spirit, because the Spirit intercedes for the saints in accordance with God's will." Romans 8:26-27 (NIV). I needed this kind of help. The pain I had lived with had been indescribable. I did not have words for the way I felt. I believed that perhaps this language would enable me to somehow tell God where I was and how I felt.

I approached one of the church ministers in November of 1994 and told her that I desired to have my own prayer language. She spoke with me briefly before she laid hands on me and prayed.

Afterward, she told me that I had to believe in my heart that God would grant me the desire of my heart. Only then would it manifest.

With the holidays approaching, the winter air began to get cold and biting. I still carried with me a lot of the issues that had pestered me throughout my entire life. Although the holidays almost always cheered me some, I was not as jubilant as I would normally have been at such a time. It would be our son's first Christmas with us. The Saturday following Thanksgiving we put up our Christmas tree. The holiday season was coming into full swing, but I was simply going though the motions.

Christmas Eve came. I had gone for a walk to the neighborhood grocery store just to get some fresh air; and my eldest daughter had accompanied me. We did not have an overabundance of money at the time, so we only got a few staples for the kitchen. As we walked back towards the house, we talked about Christmas, falling silent intermittently. I began thinking about my request for my prayer language and believing God for it. We were walking quietly when I felt something strange building inside me. I was not frightened. Oddly enough I felt comforted as the sensation became stronger. I slowed my pace and my daughter turned to look back. Suddenly, I began speaking in tongues. My daughter looked at me quizzically. I'm sure my look of surprise didn't do much to comfort her. I realized that I had been blessed with my prayer language. I hugged my daughter joyously. I stopped talking. I waited. I opened my mouth again, willing it to happen again but thinking it was just some fluke. But my prayer language came pouring out again. My daughter's curiosity got the better of her. She asked me *"Mommy, what's happening to you?"* I turned to reassure her, telling her I had just received a wonderful Christmas gift.

As we grew in the Lord, so did our challenges. My daughters had started school. The eldest had some behavior problems from the very first day of kindergarten. The school pushed for us to take her to a doctor. On average, the school was calling me to come and deal with my daughter about three times a week. As my frustration had grown, I had begun to wonder if maybe the school wasn't right. Maybe she did need some help. We took her to a psychologist and psychiatrist. The doctors had prescribed Ritalin. She had therapy a couple times a week. Yet and still, her behavior had not modified itself in the least. To the contrary, on days when we had forgotten her dosage, it seemed a convenient excuse for her to let loose with the worst behavior. She became more aggressive; and her violence began to cross boundaries that left me stunned and bewildered. She was breaking furniture, doors, and windows. She had even admitted to intentionally hurting children at school.

The psychologist recommended "hold" therapy. "Hold therapy" requires that an adult wrap their arms and legs around the child when the child is in the throes of a violent episode. You are supposed to keep holding the child firmly until the fit subsides. This was, at best, a risky proposition for us. When Leketia would begin to have one of her fits, we first had to get close enough to grab hold of her. This was hard enough. While I was holding her, she would often writhe, her body stretching out and becoming taut. Every muscle of her body would tense as the most inhuman of sounds came from her little body. The strength of her angry body would often send my head smashing against a wall or doorway behind me. My arms and legs were constantly covered in bruises. Eventually, she would tire of her tirade and collapse in a heap in my arms. We became the victims of emotional and physical battering in our efforts to employ this therapy. I had become frustrated beyond my own capability to deal with her problems. I had my own issues. I had begun tearing my hair out by the roots, nearly losing my mind in helping her deal with her issues.

One of the ministers in the church had counseled me about my daughter's behavior and how God could help us with her. We had been told that the medicine eventually becomes a crutch, giving the child an excuse to misbehave whether they had taken their dosage that day or skipped it. We had already seen that manifest. This minister advised me that we should take our daughter to the Pastor and the elders so that they could lay hands on her, pray for her and anoint her with oil. But, it would not work unless I had faith that God would work things out. I wanted my daughter to get better, so having the faith that God would heal her was easy. I saw her pain, the pain of not being able to control what she was doing. She had experienced pain caused by being rejected for her unacceptable behavior.

The Pastor laid hands on her and we all prayed for her. Her head was anointed with oil. The only thing I had to do was pray and stand firm in my faith, however little it had developed by that point. I had already taken her off the medications. After she was prayed over, there was an almost immediate turn-around in her behavior. She was far from the perfect child, but her violent fits ceased almost instantly.

I continued to grow in the Lord, and I felt God drawing me closer to Him. I would sit in service and take notes while the Pastor spoke. At times, inspiration would strike me, and I would flip to the back of my notebook and jot something down quickly. I did this so that the seeds God was planting in my life could take root. If I forgot them, they would simply die and wither away. One of our Pastor's favorite sayings has always been, "A long pencil is better than a short memory".

One day in 1999, the Pastor preached a sermon entitled "Remember Me, Lord". Towards the end of the service, the Pastor called me up to the altar. I trembled as he prophesied over me. He spoke about how people had overlooked me and ridiculed me. He spoke about how they had belittled me and made me feel as though I were nothing. He told me that everything that I had endured would be to the glory of God. He said that God would raise me up. There was no way for him to have known about all that I had been through. I had never told anyone how I felt. I had felt invisible and unworthy of love for so many years. I was convinced the words he spoke had come from God. I asked God to show me what He had for me to do. "And I will do whatever you ask in my name, so that the Son may bring glory to the Father. You may ask for anything in my name, and I will do it." John 14:13-14 (NIV)

It was not long after my prayer asking God to show me what my purpose was, that He had begun to reveal those things to me. I began to see glimpses of things to come. All I know was that I had a job to do. The phone was ringing. If I answered it, what would He say? What would I do? What would be required of me? I had so many questions, including the biggest one, with which I had the hardest time: *"Why me?"* I had never felt respected or even listened to. There were so many more people who were more capable of impacting the world than I could have been. I needed answers-- practical answers. I arranged a meeting with the very same church elder whom had prayed over me for the manifestation of my spirit language.

We sat in one of the classrooms in the Children's church area one late afternoon in June 1999. As we sat in the classroom, having prayed, I wondered where to start. How was I going to say something for which I had no words? But there was a burgeoning sense of purpose within me, so I pressed on. I related to her that I believed I had a call on my life--that God had a special purpose for me. However, I was not sure how to proceed. In coming into this meeting with her, I believed that she would lay out the steps for me and encourage me on my way. What came from her surprised me at the time, but later made perfect sense. She spoke about the awesome responsibility that comes with a call from God. She told me that when someone serves God in the ministry, they oftentimes have a full plate. If I truly believed that I had such a call on my life, I should pray fervently. God would show me the answers I sought beyond a shadow of a doubt.

I let out such a deep sigh. I was half discouraged, half confused. I listened intently as she spoke. God began to give me insight into her words and He reassured me. Somehow, I knew all she was saying was true. She related to me the amount of time she had waited and studied between hearing the call and actually answering it. I had to be absolutely sure, she had said, that I was willing to make the sacrifice such service required. In the weeks that followed, I sought God in prayer and through His scriptures. Still, oftentimes I wavered in my prayer life and bible reading. Life was always so hectic. There were so many other things I wanted to do. But I continued to hear God calling me.

Chapter 6

Breaking The Silence

"The man without the Spirit does not accept the
things that come from the Spirit of God, for they are
foolishness to him, and he cannot understand them,
because they are spiritually discerned." 1
Corinthians 2:14 (NIV)

It may seem foreign to some that I should feel led by
God to bear my soul. Some would say that it would
be contrary to the word of God to divulge certain
"private" matters. In fact, there was a "pastor"
who had told me that to do so would only glorify
the work of the enemy. But I ask you this: how
does the enemy get the glory when I have found
victory through Christ Jesus? How in the world can
others in the same situation understand they are not
alone if I remain silent? How can they understand it
is not insurmountable unless they see someone who
has overcome?

Granted, it was a long path to get to where I am today. I spent many years wallowing in a sea of self-pity and anger. I had grown to hate my father and despise my mother for all that had happened to me. It was not until we found our church home and God was able to minister to me through such a wonderful Pastor, that the healing began.

The very first thing I had to understand was that there were spiritual entities at play within my situation. The same deviant spirit that had attached itself to my father became transferred to me during our "contact". My father had never been a religious man. He despised going to church and having to wear a tie. He also did not understand what 1 Corinthians 6:13 (NIV) says: "The body is not meant for sexual immorality, but for the Lord." Perhaps he understood in his mind the concept of fidelity, but the spirit that had attached itself to him would not let him adhere to such basic principals as truth and honor. He clearly did not have an understanding of what it was that God had said about me before I had even been born. He had no concept of the lingering effects of his abuse. He had no idea how long I would suffer.

The clearest memory I have from my youth is of how I felt when I was growing up. After my father had pressed his way into a part of my life where he did not belong, I can remember a growing sense of isolation. I recall wishing someone, anyone, would figure out what was happening. I wanted to be rescued from my situation. Every stranger that came within my personal space was a possible redeemer. I felt as though I was screaming at the top of my lungs. My voiceless screams were never heard. Because of the degradation I had suffered, I became withdrawn. I felt that I was worthless, that no one would or should ever bother with me. The best analogy I can think of to give is this:

Years ago we used to have a cat. Anyone who knows about housecats knows that they need a litter box. Invariably, that litter box has to either be emptied or scooped out. With the advent of "scoopable" litter, scooping became more prevalent. I had a large black spatula that I had purchased at a local store. To see it, you would think that it would be perfect for turning pancakes or burgers and the like. After using the spatula to scoop out the cat's litter box, it was incomprehensible for me to think of this ordinary kitchen utensil being used in cooking, regardless of how many times it was washed. It could never be cleaned of the memory that it had been used to clean out the litter box.

Much in the same way that the spatula had been perverted and rendered unacceptable for its intended purpose. I felt my purpose had been perverted. I have often heard it said: If you do not understand God's intended purpose for something, you are bound to misuse it.

Spending my youth in the same household with an opportunistic father and a mother who despised me had dire consequences for my spiritual being. I learned that my opinion didn't matter and that my feelings didn't count. I learned to stuff my feelings deep down inside. All the anger I felt was shoved down--the pain was shoved down. The more I tried to push the pain down deep inside me, the bigger the vacuum became that existed in my life. The vacuum, the feeling of emptiness, of being lost, of not fitting in, began to ache unbearably.

When I had left my parent's house at the age of seventeen, joining the military, I thought I was leaving it all behind me. I was so happy, regardless of what I had to go through in order to get out of there. I was leaving!! No more stifling suffocation. I was going to be free. But the fact of the matter was that I would not be free. The very spirits that had tormented and vexed me all those years traveled with me. I did not know about them. I had no clue that I could get rid of them. I had no idea how much influence they had. All I could see was that my circumstances were about to change in a big way. I had endured to the end! My ordeal was finally over, or so I thought.

As long as external forces had control of what I did, I had managed to stay out of trouble. As long as there was someone to act as a monitor in my life, I was able to adhere to set standards. It remained that way throughout basic training. The control was still there. The true litmus test was what I would do when left to my own means on that first fateful weekend in advanced training.

Looking back, I can see now that there were spiritual influences at work. My father had a habit of drinking about a six-pack a night. At the very first opportunity, I began to drink alcohol. I didn't know anything about being intoxicated. (Mom and Dad had given up the hard liquor before we children could have ever been able to identify someone who was intoxicated). When I had finished the first beer and the buzz began to hit, oh my! I really liked the euphoric feeling. For a short period of time all of the hurt and pain I had lived with continuously had vanished. I felt happy, giddy. I was having a good time (and so were the demonic spirits).

In the months that followed, I allowed myself to journey into places that I knew I did not belong; and it was the hand of God that had preserved me. There were so many times that I had consumed enough alcohol to kill me. I would wake up in a puddle of my own vomit, wishing I had not awakened at all. But God had kept me. Even in my rebellion, He kept me. I had become so much like my father. I had come to a point where I had no boundaries to my sexual depravity. Like the old saying goes: I climbed the mountain because it was there.

All those years, in the back of my mind I kept hearing a voice. That voice softly reminded me that what I was doing was wrong. I shoved that voice down just like all the pain. I knew what I was doing was wrong. The point was, it felt good. At the risk of my own destruction, I did whatever it took to gain a fleeting moment of happiness or escape from the pain. It came to a point where I was on a quest. I had to find something to fill the ever-growing void that threatened my very existence. I didn't look back on the day before. I couldn't. If I looked back,

I would begin to despise myself even more. It became a cycle. I searched in vain in all the wrong places for an answer to my problem. I wanted to feel better. Although there might have been a momentary fix in what I had done, I invariably felt worse. It's like what they say about drinking and drugs: you can escape your problems for a little while, but when you come back down, the problems are still there, and then they are magnified by the hangover you've got.

But now I had found the key in finding a way out of the cycle in which I had been caught. Once in the ministry, I searched the scriptures occasionally, usually when my own frustration with myself had become unbearable. I began to learn about "spirits" and "demons". Learning about these things allowed me to find freedom from them. I also learned to forgive my father.

We make a conscious choice to do the wrong thing. It just doesn't happen. The old excuse *"the devil made me do it"* doesn't wash with God. The book of James tells us about temptation: "Let no one say when he is tempted, I am tempted by God, for God cannot be tempted with evil, neither tempteth any man: But every man is tempted, when he is drawn away by his own lust and enticed. Then when lust has conceived, it bringeth forth sin, when it is finished, bringeth forth death." James 1:13-15 (KJV)

Before I met the Lord, I had confronted my father about what he had done to me during my childhood. I expected a denial. A denial would have been acceptable, and would have added fuel to the fire of my anger. I would have had an excuse for my righteous indignation. However, he simply told me *"I don't know why I did those things."* Well, I learned that he was telling the truth, but only a half truth. He did not understand the spiritual influences that were at work in his life. He did not understand the catalyst that provoked him. However, he did know that it was something he wanted to do. It was something that he enjoyed. It brought him physical pleasure. It allowed him to exert control on someone he deemed a lesser being. He really did not understand the spiritual realm or just how much influence it can have on us. However much influence the spiritual realm might have, we ultimately must make the conscious decision whether or not to be swept away by our evil desires.

Please understand that I make no excuses for my father's behavior. I simply sought to understand it. There is no excuse for such a morally reprehensible thing. However, there is forgiveness. With the help of Jesus, I came to a point where I could forgive my father for what he had done. I won't say it was easy. Every bit of my flesh screamed out for me not to do so. I (the flesh) wanted to be angry at him, to make him suffer for what he had done. But I learned that carrying all that anger hurt me more than it hurt him. In the years that passed after my mother's death, God allowed me to see that my father had begun to reap the fruit of his works.

Shortly after my mother died, the phone calls and visits from relatives stopped. He began to live a life of virtual isolation. He had begun to experience the same isolation that I had known for so long. I suppose that my brothers and I were the only human contact he had, other than that of his co-workers. He ceased taking care of himself. His diabetes ran almost unchecked and was giving him gout in his feet and was taking his sight. After my mother's death, my father led a solitary and seemingly joyless life. The phone calls I made to him were difficult. He would always complain about the latest malady with which he was dealing. I tried so hard to tell him about how God had changed my life. I told him God could change things for him as well. Any time I mentioned God; he would curse at me and change the subject. His isolation and loneliness began to manifest in anger and bitterness.

He had so many complications in his physical body that when he passed, the doctors could not cite any one condition which caused his demise. He died alone and naked, lying in his own bed. Going to his funeral was painful. His body looked as though he had aged twenty-five years in the five years since my mother had died. I winced when I heard the priest praying for God to have mercy on his soul. If my father had not repented before he died, there was to be no more mercy for him.

The situation that existed for me in my childhood, coupled with my desire to deal with issues and have them out in the open had caused distance to grow between me and my brothers. I also knew with my father's passing that any relationship I might have had with my brothers would no longer exist. There was no commonality left for us then. The last real connection we had to each other was gone. It seemed to me that they were quite content not to have to deal with me or my issues.

Chapter 7

People Who Water The Garden And Help You
Weed It

*"Before I formed thee in the belly, I knew thee; and
before thou camest forth out of the womb, I
sanctified thee, and I ordained thee a prophet unto
the nations."* Jeremiah 1:5 (KJV)

As the months continued to pass, I learned more
about God's word and more about what He had for
me to do. I also learned more about his blessings. I
came to a point in my life where I no longer lived in
abject poverty. Charles and I had another baby,
Kaia Lenae. He got a good job; and we finally were
making ends meet. We had begun tithing within the
ministry once we had joined, and now saw our
income begin to grow.

Shortly after I had given birth to Kaia, one of the
ministers from the church began coming to our
apartment for bible study. We had small groups
within the ministry devised to help newer members

to learn more about God's Word. Although I found the studies fascinating, I didn't contribute very much in the beginning. I did not want my ignorance to show. I contented myself with listening quietly while attending to our daughter. Eventually, the bible study sessions came to an end. Yet, this minister, who lived in the same apartment complex as we did, continued to visit. He availed himself of our hospitality. We gladly fed and kept company with this man. We always got something in return.

Minister Scott became an almost permanent fixture in our household in the months to come. He spent holidays with us, and became like a younger brother. I was happy that my husband had someone he could talk with about anything from Star Trek to Song of Solomon.

In the beginning, I was intimidated by this man of God who spent so much time in our home. I really wasn't all the Christian I had put myself out to be. I knew he would see through the rather thin veneer. God still had a lot of work to do on me.

Somehow, I had grown to love this man, and learned to relax a bit in his presence. I began to ask questions and become more involved in conversations in general, particularly those surrounding the scriptures. When Kaia turned three years old, she and her older brother started attending school at the academy the church had started. I spent some idle time at the school office. Soon, I had found a small niche where I could serve some kind of purpose. I also could pop in on Minister Scott from time to time. We began a practice of getting together about once a month for lunch at a local restaurant. Sometimes my husband would join us, sometimes not. During these lunches we would discuss things that were going on in our lives. He had become such a lifeline for me. Our discussions surrounded our faith, the course our lives had taken, and what God had in store for us individually. These talks were spiritually uplifting for me. I learned so much from Minister Scott. The things he contributed to my life far outweigh the cost of anything I had given.

I was particularly encouraged at one of our last lunches together. Minister Scott told me that when he had first met me he didn't like me much. I knew I had not been at all likeable. Even so, that revelation still cut a bit. I suppose it was clear to him that God had quite a bit of work to do on me. He turned out to be a true friend. He stayed when others might have run. Perhaps he could see that God had a larger purpose in my life, even before I could see it. I also watched Minister Scott grow. It was evident to me that God was at work in his life, preparing him for his upcoming role within God's ministry. He also found a new joy in the form of a relationship with a young lady who would soon become his wife.

Our lunchtime sessions became less frequent. Soon enough, they were a thing of the past. But God has given me a gift in my friendship with Minister Scott. He has given me a true friend. He has always been honest and caring in dealing with me. I know he will always tell me the truth about myself. He's always been there in time of need.

Chapter 8

Finding Purpose In Gods' Kingdom

*"There is a time for everything, and a season for
every activity under heaven."*
Ecclesiastes 3:1 (NIV)

God has blessed me tremendously in placing me in
the church home in which I am planted. I have
heard the true and living word, rightly divided.
Sometimes it stings with the pain of chastisement,
sometimes it uplifts with a truly encouraging word.
I continued to thrive in the ministry. In the spring
of 2000 I had once again begun to attend corporate
prayer on a somewhat regular basis. It was during
that season that my life's journey would no longer
be a completely nebulous thing to me. Things
started to take focus. During prayer one night, the
Pastor laid hands on me and prophesied over me.
Although I was taken by surprise, I will never forget
the words he spoke: *"There are books in you. Not
just your own story, but other books as well"*.

I pondered this one for weeks. Finally, I took pen to paper and continued again to write this book. It was in the late summer that I began to realize that this book could reach out to people in positions similar to the one I had been through. I began to see that part of my purpose was to reach out and touch lives; and that I would touch lives in a different way.

However magnanimous that purpose might seem, there was an even greater purpose to my writing this book. It helped me to cope with the many issues I had tried so hard to ignore. It ministered to me in a way that nothing else could. There is no one who understands me more than God. I began to have deep revelations of how intrinsic writing it would be to my own healing process. It was a key to my own victory and growth in Christ Jesus.

In August of that year, I was prompted to go back to school. I saw a need within the ministry to reach those who could not hear. I enrolled in an interpreter training program. I studied quite a bit and some of the classes were quite challenging. I spoke with the Lord quite frequently, agonizing over the amount of work that had to be done to reach my goal. I wondered how I would manage to balance work, family and church. I scheduled classes that interfered with church functions as little as possible.

I was prompted by a need I saw within the ministry, to reach out to people who are not normally reached. Having the ability to sign would allow me to minister to those who would otherwise miss out on the fresh revelations and inspirations that had opened my eyes.

I will not tell you that I heard from God that I should attend college. The way that things began to shape up, one might be able to argue the exact opposite. I spent nearly a year and a half taking a full course load each semester. I had to attend classes in the evening, make time for homework, and somehow keep my household in one piece. At the end of the first year, I received a "Certificate of Deaf Studies" from the college. It was then that I had considered stopping college. The load had become a bit much. And then there were the voices that I heard--voices in my head that kept telling me it was a waste of time. I was nearly discouraged to the point of quitting when another of the ministers gave me wise counsel when I had shared my thoughts. She encouraged me to continue. If I had a vision, I should see the task through to completion. It was clear, by my transcript and the scholarships I had earned, that God had granted me favor. I pushed onward with my education.

Meanwhile, I was devoting as much time as I could give to working at the office at the Academy. It was not an easy task by any means. Although I had had many jobs in the past, this was the first position that ever really gave me any true joy. I found myself happy to get up in the morning (at least most days), knowing that I was making a difference. What initially began as a distraction grew into a ministry. I had become a cog in the machine that is Christian education. I did my best to play my part in this machine, to the benefit of others around me.

As I continued to grow in the ministry, God began showing me things that had to be given to Him, if I was going to heal completely. These were dark, secret things that I wanted no one to see. It seemed that I had become so comfortable carrying these things around that I didn't realize that I was carrying them. But one by one, as I grew in the Lord, I began to surrender these things to Him. It's a painful experience to rip the scabs away. There had been experiences in my life that brought the old memories back to the surface. My mother's death in 1992 triggered a bad episode.

The death of my father five years later had the memories resurfacing again. Each of these was a situation that was thrust upon me. But it was a very different story to write a book about my experiences. It was no easy task to unearth the demons that had tormented me for so long. But now, I had a new strength I had not had before. I had the strength to defeat the unearthed demons through Jesus Christ. I had the strength that God had given me. And once exposed to the light, the demons no longer held their power over me. Jesus is the light of my life!

Chapter 9

The Power Of Labels

A label tells the purchaser what the product is and the purpose of the product. A label can often have care and use instructions as well. A father who perverts the father-daughter relationship clearly does not read God's label about care, purpose and use. This label is clearly found in the Word of God. With the absence of the creator of the product in the room with you, you may not necessarily know the purpose of that thing. My father had no true knowledge of what my purpose was, because he had never read God's Word.

God has created us, and placed us within the confines of time, for a **specific purpose**. Our purpose is outlined in His word. When those around us, in particular those we trust, do not understand our purpose, they may misuse us. This is what happened with my father. He did not understand the true purpose of children, nor did he understand his role as a father. This is only part of what caused my father to abuse me. I have reason to believe that perhaps he might have been abused as a child. I also suspect that his example of a parent-child relationship had been polluted. He oftentimes would complain about his mother. He spoke about how domineering she had been. The worst part of the situation was that he did not see those traits in himself. Never having been taught otherwise, this became the pattern in his adult life. All three of us children suffered at his hands, not to mention our mother. Although he was raised in the Catholic Church, he didn't understand the purpose of life. He had no clue of destiny and purpose, and did not understand the spiritual implications of what he was doing. Even more so, I believe that my father had submitted himself to a salacious demonic spirit. It drove him because he let it.

What I heard, over the years I was under subjection of my father, programmed my thought patterns. It was so ingrained in me, it became my truth. All the little girls did this for their daddies. Obviously, this was my duty. It was no use to complain. To complain, to expose the truth, would bring about the destruction of the family. I learned that my feelings and my rights were secondary to the family around me. I felt I was stuck in this position of being the object of his deviant obsession. Even when I broke away from the home environment, thinking I was free, this mentality traveled with me.

The repercussions of my father's actions have been far reaching. Just recently, I went to visit one of my brothers to inform him of the impending release of this book. He, himself, was still searching for answers. He acknowledged and understood what had happened to me. But moreover, he was perplexed by his own state. He wondered what our parents had done to him. He, like me, has always had trouble making emotional connections. Trust is always an issue for sufferers of abuse. He questioned whether something had happened to him which might explain his own "disconnection". So far as I can recollect, he had always been the favorite son. I had never witnessed any kind of abuse directed at him. Just the same, he had been affected.

As painful as the effects of his past might have been, I believe that it has served its' purpose in his life. For as long as I can remember, he has been working within a church ministry, doing family and relationship counseling. He has been serving in ministry in some way or another since before I had graduated high school. He had found a way out of the abyss and was led to guide others to a greater freedom. I praise God for that.

The abuse that I had suffered at my parent's hands was much more severe than his. It changed who I was at the deepest levels. That day, lying in the bathtub, looking over at the toilet I had replaced, I felt so low that words cannot describe. My very soul ached. My father had turned me into a waste receptacle. He had taught me that the way to gain acceptance was to submit to the sexual desires of another. He taught me that I was something to be dumped upon. What he also taught me is that there was no one I could truly trust. The people I had trusted most to act in my best interest had let me down in a big way.

As I grew older, these thought processes became an integral part of me. I continually searched for acceptance. Since my father had accepted me and cared about me only as an object of sexual depravity, that is what I learned that I had to be as a matter of course. Every male that approached me became my next greatest hope. *Maybe this time I will find love.* Invariably, these men used me for their own purposes. I became a waste receptacle for them. They moved on, leaving me even more wounded.

This cycle of searching for acceptance and being left wounded caused a deep bitterness to grow. I began to build walls around myself to protect me from any further hurt. I hesitated to let anyone near. I became rude and abrasive, so as to keep people at arm's distance. Relationships I had were brief and shallow, serving only physical needs. Soon, I had begun to loathe myself so deeply, that I could not face myself. This is where the drinking and drug use had started.

When I finally did find a relationship, in retrospect, it is no wonder that I ended up in a relationship with Sammy, who was not unlike my father. There were so many similarities between the two of them. However, at the time I was blind. I did not see that I was merely falling into my "comfort zone". This is the kind of controlling, abusive treatment to which I had become so accustomed.

As I journeyed through life, it seemed I had the aforementioned "victim" label stamped on my forehead. I had been marked as an easy target. The salacious spirits that had governed my father's activities had transferred to me. There is a spiritual transfer which takes place during intimacy between people. The first book of Corinthians, in verse 6:16 outlines this. If a young girl begins to spend time with promiscuous women, those spirits, as well as the habits, will transfer. There was a spirit of depravity that lay within me. It had marked me as easy prey for any predator. There is a spiritual recognition that takes place. With every predator I encountered, my self-esteem slipped deeper into the abyss.

I had spent so many years at the mercy of people who had no understanding of my purpose or destiny. This was because I, myself, had no concept of who I was in God. I did not feel as though I deserved any better, regardless of how much I might have wanted better for myself. This sense way of thinking for me was so strong that, when I actually found Charles, a man who cherished and respected me, I subconsciously set out to destroy that relationship. This mentality was only exacerbated by my mother's death.

After my attempted suicide, I had come to a crossroads in my life. We had joined this ministry, and the time had come for me to come to terms with my past. I had to learn who I was and what purpose there was for me. If I did not, I was destined to repeat my self-destructive cycle once again. The time had come to break generational curses. I had to find purpose in my life.

While I am not responsible for what happened to me in my younger years, I have long since reached the age of accountability. Since that time, I have done a great many things that I would like to hide from the world. I have done so many things of which I am not proud. But with Jesus, all those things are forgiven, and I need not look back.

You must understand that none of us are worthy of Jesus' sacrifice, but all of us are worth it. So, okay, you've done some stuff. But scripture tells us "For all have sinned and fallen short of the Glory of God." Romans 3:23 (KJV) There is absolutely nothing that you could have done in your past that Jesus can't or won't forgive. The day I gave my life to the Lord was the best day of my life. Even at the moment I was praying the repentant prayer and accepting Christ, there was so much of me that I thought made me unworthy of His forgiveness, unworthy of His blood. The point is, if you are still alive, and it is in your heart to come to Christ, He will forgive. I should know.

God knew that you were going to sin. Sin is a curse. There is no escape from sin except through Christ. Jesus said "I am the way the truth and the life. No one comes to the Father except through me." John 14:6 (NIV)

Changing my circumstances did not change the way that I felt about myself. The labels I had been given by so many, I thought, had to be right. There was such a consensus. I was worthless. I could not run from the way I felt, or the labels I had accepted. The only way that I could change the course of my life and how I felt about myself, was to change the way I identified myself. I could no longer allow others to place labels on me or define me. It was necessary to go back to my creator to discover my definition.

It was after meeting God, and learning more about His love and mercy that I learned that my life had purpose. Without a doubt, some pretty terrible things happened to me in my childhood. I further exacerbated those problems with my reactionary behavior once I had left home. When I left home, I had taken all the pain, hurt, and negative labels with me. All of this caused me not to see my own value and purpose.

Perhaps the most critical message of all would be this: never allow your circumstances or other people to label you or dictate what you do. I had spent so many years believing that I was worthless and useless. The degradation that I suffered at the hands of my father placed clear identifiers on my life. It also set in place behavioral patterns which were no less than destructive. It was only God who was able to remove those labels. It was only God who was able to show me the truth about myself and allow me to find my way out of a vicious cycle of self-degrading and destructive behaviors. He did this through His word.

Through my journey of discovery, I learned that God had created me. He took care and concern to create me, and placed within me everything that I needed to rise to the challenges of my ordained purpose. Within me were the solutions to every challenge I would face. I am important to Him. I learned that He cares for me. He cares for all of His creation. He loves us so much that He sent His only son to the world so that the world through Him might be saved (John 3:16). What an awesome sacrifice! This was the kind of love and acceptance for which I had yearned.

Because of this love, God wants us to understand who we are and our purpose on this earth. He appointed certain men throughout history, and inspired them to write the scriptures. Within the bible, you will find an immense wealth of information detailing what God says about you and your purpose. What I want to share with you are some of the very basic truths that I have learned that have been the core of my healing.

Chapter 10

Back To The Beginning: Coming Back Home

"In the beginning was the Word, and the Word was with God, and the Word was God. The same was in the beginning with God. All things were made by Him, and without Him was not anything made that was made." John 1:1-3 (KJV) This scripture is the beginning to understanding who you are. You are God's creation. If we study longer, we find that there are many other scriptures that explain our beginnings, our very purposeful creation. "Before I formed thee in the belly, I knew thee; and before thou camest out of the womb, I sanctified thee; and I ordained thee as a prophet unto the nations." Jeremiah 1:5 (KJV)

These quoted scriptures together demonstrate that God had intimate knowledge of us before we existed in the flesh. We existed with Him as spirit. And after knowing us in the spirit, as a part of him (as He is our Father), He took great care in forming our physical nature. If you think of the miraculous process which takes place following the moment of conception, you can begin to comprehend the diligent care God has taken in "knitting you together" in the flesh.

In Psalms 139:14 (NIV) the psalmist, David, says: "I praise you because I am fearfully and wonderfully made; your works are wonderful, I know that full well." You are fearfully and wonderfully made. How deeply God cares for you, that He has numbered the hairs on your head (Matthew 10:30). Each and every one of us is important to God, as He outlines in Matthew 18:14 (KJV): "Even so it is not the will of your father which is in heaven that one of these little ones should perish".

He does not want us to perish nor live a life separate from Him. In knowing Him, and having a covenant relationship with Him, we can discover who it is we are--by His definition. Only then can we live up to the full potential God placed within us before we were even born. Do you want to know Him? Do you want to discover your purpose? The first step is to pray for forgiveness and ask Jesus into your heart. You can do that right now! Scripture tells us that if we believe in our hearts, and confess with our mouths, that Jesus is Lord and that God raised Him from the dead, we shall be saved (Romans 10:19). Pray this prayer with me:

Lord Jesus, I need You. I believe that God sent you and that You died on the cross for me. I believe that God raised You from the dead. I have sinned against You. Lord Jesus, forgive my sins, blot out my iniquities, and create in me a clean heart. Come into my heart Jesus, and be Lord of my life. I give my life to You. I thank You and praise You for this time of new beginnings. I ask You to stay with me to strengthen me and guide me. I give You all glory and honor. In Jesus name, Amen.

Now is the time when, as a new creature, you can truly begin to change your life for the better. It is time to grow. You will serve your growth process greatly by surrounding yourself with those who will edify you and build you up.

Those who will encourage you and rejoice in your victories are your greatest allies. Find yourself in a church body where you can hear the word rightly divided among people of like mind. People there are more likely to encourage you in your Christian walk. If you ask God to show you where to go, He will lead you in your search.

Many people have the misconception that being born again fixes every problem you have in your life. And others who have had negative experiences in churches may have a less than favorable view of Christianity. They may have had contact with misled people who confessed to be Christians, but who treated them badly. They mistakenly believe that all Christians act in the same manner. Therefore their propensity is to shy away from religion. However, true Christians make a daily effort to grow in their abilities to treat others as Christ treated people. It doesn't mean we're perfect; it simply means we are forgiven.

As I have said previously, none of us are worthy of the blood of Christ, but Christ counted us all worth the greatest of all sacrifices. No matter what it is that you have done in the past, God can forgive you.

What you really may struggle with, as I did, is **will** God forgive *you*? It was easy for me to be happy for someone else over the joy they felt at being born again; but I was sure that they could not have been as bad as I had been. I felt that I was so corrupted and evil that even God could not forgive me. But I learned that if you still have breath in your body, it is not too late to ask for forgiveness. God is faithful and He will forgive.

When you find a church home, do not expect every person within the congregation to embrace you. That would be an ideal situation, but every person on earth is subject to the flesh. We all have our attitudes and preconceived notions. And you will never win everyone over. You will always have critics. There are even people like you—newly born again. There may be some there that are unsaved. But then again, the only important opinion is that of God. If you are living your life in accordance with the scriptures, and journeying closer to Him, He will sustain you.

If you are trying to hard to win over others and be accepted, it's time to take as step back. Perhaps you are still walking with the mentality that you have to please others. It's nice to have friends. That much is true. But you should never devalue yourself in order to find them. Simply be who you are. You are a work in progress. You are continually evolving. Keep your focus on God and His word.

Here is what invariably happens. Those who you associated with before meeting Jesus and making these changes in your life may begin to look at you rather scornfully. They may not like the changes. They may make accusations that you think you are better than them. Let me warn you—do not let this deter you.

When this happens, you will find it necessary to change the company you keep. People who speak negatively about you are not your friends. You will need to make a clean break from these toxic people. "Do not be misled. Bad company corrupts good character." 1 Corinthians 15:33 (NIV) Read further with Paul in 2 Corinthians, chapter two: "If you have any encouragement from being united with Christ, if any comfort from His love, if any fellowship with the Spirit, if any tenderness and compassion, then make my joy complete by being like-minded, having the same love, being one in spirit and purpose. Do nothing out of selfish ambition or vain conceit, but in humility consider others better than yourselves." (vss 1-3)

Other than your greater purpose in His kingdom, you may have other talents and abilities. Find a ministry within that church body in which you can put those talents to use. Believe me when I say that you will gain so much more than you give in doing so. You will be able to get to know people a bit more intimately. In working in ministry, you are setting down roots. You are saying "This is where I belong". Becoming a part and being accountable to others makes you much less likely to walk away hurt if someone offends you.

Let's address those labels once again. Labels are great for food products, to let you know how much something costs, to tell you what kind of fabric that new suit is made of and how to care for it. But the thing that you have to remember is: Who put the labels on those products? Most usually, the person who cooked the food, made the garment, or purchased the product wholesale. And here is the key—they have knowledge about the product. They know what went into making it. They also know the intended purpose of the item at hand. What about you? Who made you? Some might say their parents. But if you know the truth, as I do, you will have to say that God created you. He created you with a **specific design and purpose**. You came from Him. He has numbered your days (Job 14) and put within in you every capacity your life will require you to draw upon.

As I have outlined in citing John 1:1-3, God created us. As our creator, He is the supreme authority as to the purpose of His creation. He understands our purpose better than any other person ever could. If someone does not know your purpose, they are bound to mistreat you. And furthermore, if you do not understand your own purpose, you will allow others to mistreat you, because you do not know any better. If people consistently treat you in a manner inconsistent with your purpose, you can wander farther from that purpose. This inevitably becomes your comfort zone.

If you are feeling worthless, walking around with labels that others have given you, I want to offer you hope. You no longer have to accept those labels. The people who have labeled you have not created you. They cannot understand the purpose that our Father has placed in you. If you search His Word, you will find so many occasions where God speaks of your value. How highly He esteems you!

He knows your heart. And like Solomon, if you ask for wisdom, it will be given and everything else comes along (2 Chronicles 1:11-12). Besides, people get hurt when mislabeling occurs.

This is why I say no one should be allowed to label you. They do not understand what your purpose is, or why God created you a certain way. So there really is no way they can know enough about you to label you. You must stop accepting labels from others. Read God's word and find out for yourself what He says about you.

How do we get rid of those negative labels mistakenly assigned to us by others? It's not enough to reject the label and tear it off. You must find something with which to replace it. Find a deeper relationship with Him to the extent where He becomes part of your daily life. In doing so, you change how you are programming yourself. This can help you to change the habits which may have contributed to your negative labeling. Additionally, you can ask Him about your purpose.

What is your God-ordained purpose in life? Everything that God creates has a purpose. With that assignment, God has also given you instructions (biblical and prophetic), and a solution to a specific problem. I have often heard it said that God will take the very thing that He has delivered you from and turn it into an awesome ministry. If you've been there before, you can lead the way out.

In order to utilize your past experiences, you have to get past the pain of those experiences. This, too, is where Jesus is your answer. Having accepted Him as Lord and Savior, you will learn to slowly open up areas of your life to Him so that He can heal you. But Jesus is very much the gentleman. He will never force his way into any area of your life. You have to freely surrender them. You offer to Jesus the broken parts of your life much like a child offers a broken toy to a parent to fix. This child knows, with all certainty, that his parent can fix the toy. He might have even fought to fix it himself. Maybe he is frustrated with his own inability to fix the toy. But he knows that the parent can fix the toy, and will—out of love for the child.

This is how Jesus wants us to come to Him. "And verily I say unto you, except ye be converted, and become as little children, ye shall not enter into the kingdom of heaven." Matthew 18:3 (KJV) He wants to fix our broken places. It was Jesus who taught me about forgiveness. It was not until I found the Lord that I was able to forgive my father for what he had done. I learned that in forgiving him, I gained peace. I finally regained control of my emotional state. As long as I harbored anger toward him, he had the control. When I forgave him, I took back control.

Yet again, forgiveness is the bridge to Jesus. Matthew 6:14 (NIV) says "For if you forgive men when they sin against you, your heavenly Father will also forgive you". I understood that forgiving my father was the only way that my Father would forgive me. My own aught against my father could have kept me from seeing the Kingdom. As hard as it might seem, you really do need to forgive those who have wronged you.

It does not matter if the offender has not accepted this forgiveness. Don't wait for an emotional or teary response when you offer forgiveness. It is about your own freedom and release. Offering forgiveness may not even make that relationship better. The relationship that will benefit, however, is your relationship with God. When you begin to ask Jesus to forgive things as they are called to your remembrance, it may not be easy. But if you can open yourself up and surrender your hurts and your issues to Him, He will heal you. You cannot forget the things that happened to you. But Jesus is like an anesthesiologist. You know you've been through something, you have the scars to show for it, but the pain is a distant memory.

Another hurdle you may find yourself stumbling on is whether or not He can use you. Scripture tells us that God often uses the simple to confound the wise (1 Corinthians 1:27). If you have what may be considered a checkered past, God can use it. You've been forgiven. God can take the very thing that you've been delivered from and turn it into something awesome. You only have to be willing to surrender everything to Him. Everything has value to God, because God doesn't make junk.

As bad as a thing that could happen to you, God can turn your circumstances around. No matter how others might despitefully use you, God can and will turn it around. I find encouragement in Genesis and the story of Joseph, Jacob's son. Joseph was his father's favorite son because he had been born to him in his old age. His father had given Joseph a coat of many colors. This caused envy to stir within his brothers.

To make matters worse, Joseph had shared with his brothers a dream he had had. His brothers' grain heads would bow down to his. This dream only increased their anger and they plotted to get rid of him. His father had sent him to check on his brothers one day. It was at that time that they seized the opportunity to deal with him. They stripped him of his robe and threw him in a cistern. Rather than kill him, at Reuben's prodding, they sold Joseph as a slave to some Ishmaelites who were traveling to Gilead.

As the story continues, we see Joseph in a prominent position in Pharaoh's house. Because of dreams he had had regarding an impending famine, Joseph had advised Pharaoh to build storehouses for grain in preparation for the famine. Joseph was later entrusted to build up Pharaoh's storehouse. Then, as Joseph had said, the famine did indeed come. Joseph tended to the affairs of distributing grain to all those who needed. And so Joseph's other dream came to pass, where his brothers did indeed come to him, in need of grain, and bowed down to him.

What a wonderful thing Joseph did! He did not lord it over them, or tell them "I told you so". What he did was quite to the contrary. He could hardly contain himself. He wanted to hug his brothers. When they realized that he was their brother, they were fearful. I am quite sure that they feared retribution for what they had done in selling their brother into slavery. In Genesis 50:20 we see not only Joseph's love and mercy, but his understanding of God's divine plan. He tells his brothers, "You intended to harm me, but God intended it for good to accomplish what is now being done, the saving of many lives".

In many ways I feel akin to Joseph. I went through a great deal in my younger years. It could very well have destroyed me—it nearly did. Yet those things that the enemy had intended to destroy my life and my very sanity, God has turned around. I know now that God has had his hand on my life. Through the grace, mercy, and love of Jesus, I have been able to heal from the past hurts and use my healing and my testimony to help others. It is His healing power that enables me to use my testimony. What was meant to destroy me, God has turned around.

If you prayed the prayer of salvation outlined earlier in this chapter, and believed it in your heart, you are born again and have found the way. You have found the truth. God is trustworthy in all of His ways. Where others have lied to you or hurt you, by His nature, God cannot. Numbers chapter 23, verse 19 (NIV) says "God is not a man that he should lie, nor a son of man, that he should change his mind. Does he speak and then not act? Does he promise and not fulfill?" Indeed not! The truth is quite to the contrary.

Scripture tells us that He watches over His word to perform it so that it does not come back void. What He says in His Word, (or prophetically through the man of God that has been placed in your life) He will do. You only need to believe. You have to have faith that God can and will do what he says. Prophecies given to you by your pastor or minister are conditional on that same faith.

The bottom line is that God loves you so much. He is watching over you. God is omniscient. He knows everything already. There is nothing that happens in this world without God knowing about it. He has His eye on everything. He cares for you so much. He knows that you have been through something that may have hurt you deeply. Whatever that thing you have endured may be, He can take those circumstances and turn them around. "For we know that all things work together for the good to him that loves the Lord and is called according to His purpose." Romans 8:28 (NIV) God will take those things that were intended to harm you and use them for His glory.

It is necessary to get to a point in your life where you feel like you are worth the effort and love it requires to change the previous parameters of your life. Becoming born again is only the first step, but the right one. Now that you have accepted Christ, you need to open your heart and your life to Him. As you are willing to allow Christ into areas of your life, surrender those things to Him; He can begin to make things better.

When you accept Jesus as your Lord and Savior, you become a new creature. But, like getting married and taking on the title of spouse, becoming born again does not change your life situation instantly. Yes, if you are in Christ, you are a new creature (2 Corinthians 5:17). Your sins are forgiven. You have a new start, an opportunity for your life to move in a new direction. But your life still has the issues and challenges it had before becoming born again. So, where do you go from there?

Once you are born again, you must find yourself in a place that will equip you with the tools to live a Christian life. Now is the time to find a place where people are gathering together to be perfected. You need to find yourself a church where you can fellowship with other Christians and where you can hear the word of God rightly divided. The purpose of Gods' church is the perfecting of the Christian walk. None of the members is perfect or complete, so you need not be intimidated in going. It will be well worth the effort when you find a group of people who can encourage you in the Word of God.

I struggled so much with this point as a new Christian. I had accepted Christ and begun a new life, but there was so much I was holding onto. Because of my self-esteem issues, I was hesitant to open my life to Christ, although I had invited Him into my heart. In addition to that, I still suffered from an abrasive personality. This kept people from getting close and kept me from being readily accepted. The sense of inclusion I sought was slow in coming. And although I had a new friend and confidant in Christ, it was quite an abstract concept in the beginning. I had begun to grasp the concept in my mind, but my heart was a long time in catching on. And it was my heart that was hurting the most.

Now that I am learning what God says about me; the old labels are being peeled off. In my fathers' mind, the purpose for a daughter was much different than God's purpose for a daughter. However, my true purpose as defined by God had not changed. My father's perception of a father-daughter relationship eventually changed my perception of it as well. Father, Daddy, and Dad became dirty words to me. A father was someone I could not trust. A father was someone who hurt me. A father was a predator. That was the label of father in my mind.

If you have spent years, even decades, at the hands of people that treat you as though your life has no value, it's time to change the company you keep. These people do not understand that your life has purpose and value. And let me point out that you cannot simply "run away". When you leave someplace, you are going into another place. It is not enough to decide to leave where you are, but you must know where you are going. Otherwise, you end up exchanging one manner of pain for another. This is what happened to me. I yearned so much to leave my parent's house. I was so consumed with thoughts of getting out, that I gave no thought to where I was going. Eventually, I ended up in a series of relationships where I was treated much in the same manner as my father had treated me.

Until you come to a point where you know that you deserve better, you will continue to seek out your "comfort zone". This mindset must be broken. The love of Christ is the key to breaking this cycle of self-defeating behavior. It most certainly saved me.

In his book, *God Wants You Healthy, Wealthy, and Full Of Life*, Dr. Mikel Brown tells us that "people define who they are by what they do, where they are from, or by the associations they have with organizations or other people". All of these factors can have either positive or negatives affects in your life. What you need is the truth.

Once you begin to learn the things that God says about you, and accept them as truth in your life, you will begin to change the way you think about yourself. Your changing thought patterns will allow you to begin removing labels that others have *mistakenly* assigned to you. If you study His word to see what He (your creator) says about you, you can further change your thought patterns. These thought pattern changes will begin to reflect in your behavior and attitudes about yourself.

Let's discuss those labels a bit more. Have people called you ignorant or worthless? Perhaps they simply treated you as though your opinion didn't matter. Maybe they thought you weren't very smart, or you wore the wrong clothes. Whatever their criticisms, it is your decision and only your decision to accept or reject their opinion. The best way to negate those negative opinions is to find a source of positive ones. The bible is the greatest source of positive opinions about you that exists.

Once again I remind you that in His word we are told that God created us; we existed with Him in spirit before he formed us in the flesh. His words for Jeremiah are true for you as well: "For I know the plans I have for you," declares the LORD, "plans to prosper you and not to harm you, plans to give you hope and a future." Jeremiah 29:11 (NIV)

Those who mistakenly placed those labels on you sought to steal from you your hope. As you read His word, you will find more encouraging scriptures. As you read about the wonderful things God says about you, you will begin to understand that those previous labels do not apply any longer. You can replace them with the labels God intended for you to have. You are righteous, through Christ. If you are born again, you are holy. In its' simplest form, this means you are separated from the world because of your belief and your Christian walk. You are holy because God is holy (Lev 20:26), and you are His.

Change What You Know: Where you are in life is in direct correlation to your level of knowledge. For example: If you do not have the knowledge or ability to perform brain surgery, you cannot become a brain surgeon. Consequently, your income level is tied directly to your knowledge as well.

Additionally, if you do not know that you have value, you will not treat yourself as though you have value. If you are accustomed to abuse and oppression, that becomes your comfort zone. Kindness, love, and trust are foreign concepts to you. It is critical that you change your knowledge base. You need to understand what God says about you. In His word, God tell us that we are fearfully and wonderfully made (Psalms 139:14), and that God formed us in the womb (Isaiah 44:24). You have a value far above rubies.

Monitor your ears! As a child of God, you have to be careful who you allow to speak into your life. Everyone you have ever met, and every experience you have ever had has had a part in defining your life. Where you are in life is a direct result of the information that you have taken in. If you have had people speaking negative words to you repeatedly, you will begin to believe those things. In my life, this was the pattern. The way my father perverted the relationship God intended us to have had a hand in determining how I would react to the world and the people around me.

Proverbs 18:21 (NIV) tells us that "The tongue has the power of life and death, and those who love it will eat it's fruit". What you are is partially a product of what you hear and what you say about yourself. If the maltreatment is severe enough, as it was in my own case, it can disturb your self-esteem. Gradually, you begin to accept what others say about you. Sooner or later you begin to reflect those things. Eventually, it becomes part of the fabric of your being and you project it. I had a reputation, and other labels that people had given me.

If you praise God for all that you have (the function of your body, a place to live, and for something as simple has how He made you), and allow His praise to continually be in your mouth, your have the power to change your life. As the praises go up, the Blessor comes down.

Praise is also essential in another way: it confuses the enemy. He is doing his best to wreak havoc in your life. In praising God, even through difficult circumstances, you remove power from the devil's hands. Change what you say in reaction to the things that happen in your life and the way people treat you by using positive words. Glorifying God and giving Him praise are the most positive words that can come from your mouth. Remember the power of the tongue! Most importantly, remember the power in the name of Jesus, your savior!

I became increasingly blessed when I really started studying the Word. I began to see in the bible what God had made me to be. After so many years of being defined by others and how they treated me, I found a new, truer definition of who I am. I learned that I am fearfully and wonderfully made, that my worth is far beyond my own imagination. I learned that I have a purpose, because everything that God has created has purpose (Ecclesiastes 3:1).

In order to reconstruct your life, you have to take time seeking God. It is critical that you seek Him and ask Him to show you what parts of your life your need to surrender. You have to get rid of all the excess negative baggage with which you entered this new life. This baggage only weighs you down and hinders your growth process.

It is extremely important that you are willing to surrender these things to God. God is a gentleman and will not force His way in. He will not take from you what you are holding on to. It is only with willing surrender that God can begin to reconstruct your life

It has taken about eight years to get this book to print. There were so many times when I thought that I was wasting my time. The enemy had begun to plant thoughts in my mind about how futile such an effort would be. *No one would ever read the book. It would never get published. And so what if it did—it would sit on the shelves and collect dust.* And what if that did happen? If all it ever did was sit on shelves and collect dust, it would have still served a very important purpose. Writing this book has been the best therapy. It has been instrumental in my own healing process.

Jesus is the reason why I am strong enough to tell my story. He is the reason why I am still here today and not buried six feet under. It is His salvation and love that have carried me through. I admonish you to seek the Lord. Find Him. Invite Jesus in your heart and confess your sins—this very moment. Tomorrow is not promised. Jesus waits for you to ask Him into your life. Repent and ask Him to strengthen you so that you can live a sanctified life. He loves you so much that He willingly died on the cross for your sins, so that you might find eternal life (John 3:16). He then conquered death by rising from the grave. He did this all for you. But you have to decide to invite Him in and ask for His forgiveness.

I know that it is His forgiveness of my own sins that helped me learn how to forgive. Because He forgave me, I was able to forgive my parents for the things that happened in the past. I have also learned to forgive myself. It is His mercy and grace that have taught me to have mercy on others. He is the way to eternal life.

God has been speaking through His Word, hoping that you will seek Him and find His love. Whatever it is you've been through, whatever it is you've done—He can and will forgive you if you ask. He can take any bad situation and turn it around for your good. He loves you so much that he does not want you to life a life of despair. He does not want you to continue to carry the pain and excess baggage of your old life. He stands with open arms, waiting for you to find Him. He is found by those who seek Him. Search Him out. Find Him who knows your purpose and destiny. Lean your ear to his mouth. Lean your mouth to His ear. Let him wrap His loving arms around you. There is safety and comfort in His embrace. Come back to daddy. Daughter, come home.

About The Author

Deborah Babers is a devoted wife and mother of four children who has dedicated her life to helping meet the educational and emotional needs of children. For the last six years, she has been a full-time volunteer at Christian Joy Center Preschool and Academy, a bible-based private school in El Paso, Texas. She has provided sign language interpreting for the deaf within the church environment. For the past five years, she has volunteered her time as a Guardian Ad-Litem with Court Appointed Special Advocates (CASA) of El Paso. In this capacity, she has given a voice to abused and/or neglected children within the family court system. Her early life experiences make her uniquely qualified to address the subjects of child abuse, sexual victimization, respect, and self-esteem related issues.

www.ingramcontent.com/pod-product-compliance
Lightning Source LLC
Chambersburg PA
CBHW031850090426
42741CB00005B/431